Joyful Teaching and Learning in the Primary School

Joyful Teaching and **Learning** in the Primary School

Edited by Denis Hayes

LearningMatters

Acknowledgements

The authors are pleased to acknowledge Ron Knott as the copyright holder of the photographs of the flowers in Chapter 12 and refer the reader to the following website where many more ideas on Fibonacci numbers can be found: http://www.mcs.surrey.ac.uk/personal/R.Knott/Fibonacci/.

With thanks to the staff and pupils of St Nicholas School, Sidmouth for their work relating to *My Other Granny* and to the staff and pupils of Drake's Primary School, East Budleigh for their work relating to *The Pied Piper* in Chapter 11.

The publishers would like to acknowledge Faber and Faber for kind permission to print the extract of Ted Hughes poem 'The Snail' on page 91.

First published in 2007 by Learning Matters Ltd.

British Library Cataloguing in Publication Data
A CIP record for this book is available from the British Library.

ISBN 978 1 84445 122 7

Cover design by Topics. Text design by Code 5.
Project Management by Deer Park Productions, Tavistock, Devon
Typeset by Pantek Arts Ltd, Maidstone, Kent
Printed and bound in Great Britain by Bell & Bain Ltd, Glasgow

Learning Matters Ltd
33 Southernhay East
Exeter EX1 1NX
Tel: 01392 215560
info@learningmatters.co.uk
www.learningmatters.co.uk

Contents

Introduction

Denis Hayes

When you decided to become a teacher were you motivated by the thought of becoming a slick, grey-suited government employee or a free-thinking, liberated educator? Did you sign up to be a teacher rather than (say) a civil servant or a lawyer because you wanted to spend hours on paperwork and form-filling or because you wanted to experience the joy of seeing 'the light come on' when children understand something and revel in the exhilaration that comes from sharing your time, enthusiasm and energy helping children to make sense of the world and find their place in it? Don't tell me! I think I know the answer.

The recent past has seen the emergence of an objectives-driven education system, saturated with targets, criteria, tests and league tables. The emphasis on 'performance' has threatened to, and sometimes succeeded in, stifling creativity, innovativeness and the elation that should accompany teaching and learning. More recently the government has accepted that too much of the formal curriculum and prescribed teaching methods are 'joyless' rather than 'joyful' and promoted new initiatives to (in their words) 'drive up standards' – but do we *really* want children and school staff to feel 'driven' in this way?

These central initiatives to enhance creativity and innovative practice have tended to be in the form of *appendages* to the curriculum, taking the form of (for example) a whole-school arts, science or literature week, rather than necessarily being at the heart of the regular teaching programme. While these additional learning experiences have, for the most part, been appreciated and valued by the children and staff, the underlying challenge is to lift *regular* teaching out of the 'identify objectives/plan/resource/deliver/assess/adjust your approach' model – which represents the 'mechanics' of teaching but not the artistry of it – and fashion circumstances in which even ordinary lesson content can generate more excited anticipation and enjoyment among teacher and taught. Such a dynamic situation will be characterised by a combination of carefully prepared ideas and spontaneous threads to create a joyful working environment that motivates children, with the inevitable positive impact on formal standards of achievement.

The approach described above is posited on a belief that the process of raising standards is not rooted solely in a desire to gain higher test scores but, crucially, in the enthusiasm for learning it elicits in pupils, coupled with the joy of teaching the subject or subject area experienced by teachers.

Joyful Teaching and Learning in the Primary School will be of greatest interest to trainee teachers and is based, as the title suggests, on a belief that the mechanistic, objectives-driven route to pupil achievement can and should incorporate a more spontaneous, learner-centred element. Teachers and pupils alike need a spring in their step and a belief that learning is not solely about the predictable but the unpredictable, and that the curriculum is less about 'covering' than about 'uncovering' storehouses full of priceless knowledge.

This book combines, in a readable form, practice and theory about the joys of teaching and learning, offering both a subject-orientated and thematic view of ways in which teaching and learning can be enjoyable and enjoyed. It offers an alternative view of achieving high standards by *inspiration* as much as by *perspiration*! The philosophy of the book is rooted in a comment made by Susan Isaacs more than 75 years ago:

The children themselves are the living aim and end of our teaching. It is their thought, their knowledge, their character and development, which make the purpose of our existence as schools and teachers. And it is the modes of their learning and understanding, their physical growth and social needs, which in the end determine the success or failure of our methods of teaching. (1932, p11)

Joyful Teaching and Learning in the Primary School touches on the interactive relationship between teacher and children. It aims to demonstrate how it is the birthright of all children and the entitlement of every teacher to be empowered to exercise their latent creativity and inventiveness. You will be guided in your thinking and planning by the use of case studies, diagrams, key quotations, issues to think about and reflect upon, and action points relevant to classroom practice.

Every contributor to this book is passionate about the need to rekindle a deep love of and *for* learning in our schools. We feel confident that you will find the book uplifting, useful and – we most sincerely hope – joyful!

Denis Hayes

Reference

Isaacs, S. (1932) *The Children We Teach*. London: University of London Press.

Notes on contributors

All the contributors work for the Faculty of Education, University of Plymouth and share a passion for innovative and joyful teaching and learning.

John Berry spent over forty years as an academic in higher education and since 1991 has been Professor of Mathematics. He is now enjoying a part-time role as a research professor supervising graduate students; leading mathematics workshops for gifted and talented pupils; playing golf; gardening; singing in Wells Cathedral (God songs) and enjoying his first grandson.

John Burnett taught in primary schools before working as a class teacher in a Steiner school, taking classes of children through from the age of six to fourteen years. For the past fifteen years he has been supporting students as they prepare for teaching in Steiner schools. He loves gardening, literature and fell-walking with his two sons. His particular research interest is in spirituality in education.

Suanne Gibson completed her PhD 'middle management and the role of the SENCO' at Oxford Brookes University in 2002. She has publications in the field of special educational needs and currently works as programme director on the BA education studies degree.

Denis Hayes has worked in five schools, including two as deputy head and one as a head teacher. Since moving into Higher Education he has developed a particular interest in the school experiences of trainee teachers and creative teaching strategies. Denis finds joy in singing, walking his dogs and lay preaching, and has published numerous education texts.

Joanna Haynes is a qualified primary teacher, who taught in Glasgow and Bristol before moving to Devon to work in higher education. She has worked with all age groups in different settings: nurseries, schools, community, adult education, teacher training, continuing professional development. Joanna has published articles and books on philosophy with children and has been involved in contributing to conferences and running courses, inset days and thinking events for pupils over the past twelve years.

Rachael Hincks is a former assistant head teacher, with particulaar interests in science teaching and inclusive education, including working with pupils with special educational needs and English as an additional language. In her spare time, Rachael enjoys cookery, relaxing at the beach and spending large amounts of time at the Eden Project.

Peter Kelly is Senior Lecturer on the integrated Masters Degree progamme. He was formerly head teacher of two schools in South West England – an inner city middle school and a small primary school. He has published widely on educational issues.

Helen Knowler is an experienced primary practitioner and former advisory teacher supporting pupils who have social, emotional and behavioural difficulties. She is particularly interested in the professional development of teachers, teaching identity and the use of writing to develop critically reflective practice. Joy is food, books and learning!

Bill Leedham was formerly head of Devon LEA learning resource services, and has been a teacher, governor, parent and lecturer, as well as a provider of in-service training. He is also an educational consultant and illustrator and has a web-site – www.autolycos.co.uk – which provides free access to a range of resources and ideas for the teaching of history.

Jeff Lewis taught in mainstream and special schools before entering higher education. He has written widely in the fields of special needs, behaviour, philosophy and personal, social and health education. Despite recent trends in Education, he remains optimistic.

Margaret Mackintosh is a former primary teacher, who edited the Geographical Association's magazine 'Primary Geographer' for ten years. Wherever she travels, particulary in the Scottish highlands and islands and in developing countries, she takes a sketch book and paint box to record her experiences.

Mike Murphy taught in London schools where he enjoyed promoting history as alive and well. As a SENCO and deputy head teacher he has been involved in writing and publishing curriculum materials for primary and secondary pupils. When not 'undercover' in Cornwall he is a tutor on an integrated Masters Degree programme.

Linda Pagett has worked as a primary school teacher, and is deeply interested in creative approaches to teaching and learning, especially in the field of English. Her work in the field of performance peotry has been a focus for her publications.

Nick Pratt has worked in the mathematics education team since 1994. After a degree in Engineering he has since discovered that maths is more than just a tool to achieve a job. His interest is in how teachers can be helped to see the many fascinating insights it offers and how this affects the teaching and learning in their classrooms.

Tony Rea leads the outdoor education module on the BA degree in education studies and outdoor learning modules on an integrated Masters Degree programme. He has researched many aspects of outdoor learning and has written widely about these. In his spare time he enjoys travel, hill walking and sailing.

Janet Rose is a lecturer on both the Early Childhood Studies route for the BEd and the BA. Prior to this she worked as a teacher and researcher. Her research interests centre around the role of the adult in children's learning. For the rest of the time she is joyfully raising two young children.

Arthur Shenton has worked in primary, middle and secondary schools in England and Wales as a teacher of English, and in a number of senior management roles. He currently is delighted to have the opportunity to indulge his passion for reading and children's literature as the team leader for language and literacy at the University of Plymouth.

Emma Sime originally trained as a primary school teacher with a specialism in physical education and has taught in a number of primary schools throughtout Devon. Through her work as team leader for PE at the University of Plymouth she is developing her interest in the impact that trainee teachers' experiences of the subject can have on their future practice. When not working she is extremely busy raising a young family.

Sue Waite enjoys engaging in educational research across a range of issues with affect as an overarching theme. She is particularly interested in the role of emotions and feelings in outdoor learning and pedagogy. A positive approach and the importance of enjoyment underpin all aspects of her life.

1
Teaching joyfully
Denis Hayes

Introduction

Some years ago I worked with a colleague who was sceptical about the claim that effective teaching depended in large measure on the level of inspiration and the strength of relationships between teacher and pupils. He argued that parents merely wanted their children to be taught by someone who was well-informed, would get them through their tests and exams as quickly as possible and prepare them for secondary school. Most of us involved in primary education (indeed, *any* form of education) might be uneasy about such a mechanistic view of education:

> Get them in → Get them taught → Get them through their exams → Move them on to the next stage

Yet my colleague was only expressing what some politicians and educationists have been claiming for years, namely that the teacher's job is to provide children with subject knowledge and opportunities to master the formal curriculum so that they can be groomed for success in the plethora of national tests they will have to face during the school years. Governments have staked their reputations on improved results and spent considerable amounts of public money to 'drive up standards'. Alongside the euphoria, however, deep concerns have been expressed about the pressure that satisfying these external demands places on teachers and children and the curriculum impoverishment that results. The strength of these counter-arguments is already having a positive effect on government thinking; they have led to much greater attention being paid to the significance of creativity and experiential learning. Good news!

Every survey about primary teachers' motivation concludes that they not only want their pupils to do well academically but also to mature socially, emotionally and spiritually. This desire is reflected in the way that teachers speak of 'my children' rather than 'our pupils' and talk endlessly about children who delight them or cause them concern. If two or more teachers meet they will agree not to talk about school and end up doing precisely that! Being a teacher really is a way of life, as you will quickly discover. But there's much more to being a teacher than 'delivering' a lesson. Read on.

Becoming a qualified teacher

A generation ago the majority of primary school teachers were trained in teacher training colleges that were designed specifically for that purpose. Student teachers spent blocks of time in school (a period referred to as 'teaching practice') supervised by a tutor from the college. The role of the host school was principally to provide placement opportunities for the students to practise and hone their classroom teaching skills.

Over recent years the situation has changed markedly. First, preparation for teaching has shifted from an emphasis on *educating* student teachers (encouraging them to develop their own educational priorities) to one of *training* (inculcating into them centrally imposed priorities), with strings of national targets attached to classroom practice and school membership (known as 'standards') that have to be met. Second, this change of emphasis has resulted in a change of vocabulary, such that student teachers are more often referred to as 'trainee teachers' or 'trainees', and for simplicity these terms will be employed throughout the remainder of this chapter. Third, the dominance of the old teacher training colleges in preparing new teachers has been replaced by an active partnership with schools. Fourth, time in schools not only offers opportunities for trainees to practise their teaching but also to gain experience of the varied aspects of school life outside the immediacy of the classroom: planning, staff meetings, extra-curricular activities, parent meetings and dealing with external agencies (such as social workers) as part of the Every Child Matters (ECM) agenda.

Schools involved in preparing new teachers are expected to provide programmes through which trainees are timetabled to meet with key persons in the school (e.g. subject leaders, special educational needs coordinators/SENCOs), to 'shadow' staff undertaking different roles, such as observing an experienced teacher in PE or working alongside a teaching assistant who is supporting an autistic child, and to attend relevant meetings, such as curriculum workshops and discussions about implementing the latest government initiative.

The school-based training programme allows you to learn from and offer ideas during curriculum meetings, share your own expertise with colleagues and contribute to wider school activities, such as sports days, fetes, educational visits and special events (e.g. an arts or science week). It pays to immerse yourself in these experiences as deeply as you can, as once qualified there always seem to be other pressing priorities that require attention.

The role of tutors from the training-providing establishment (commonly a university faculty of education) tends to be as much one of facilitator and guardian of standards as advising trainees about classroom and professional practice, a task increasingly undertaken by the host teachers. A school-based tutor, often known as *the mentor*, liaises with the university tutor, oversees the trainee teacher's progress and makes judgements about the final grades. In addition to the mentor's comments, the class teacher and other host teachers frequently provide verbal or written feedback to trainees about the quality of their classroom work and contribution to school life. You therefore have access to advice and support from at least four sources.

- **the tutor from the training-provider;**
- **the tutor (mentor) in the school;**
- **the class teacher;**
- **other colleagues.**

Most trainees benefit considerably from this reservoir of expertise, though some find mediating the various views and attitudes of the different advisers to be a challenge. Trainee teachers not only have to satisfy the criteria for competence ('fulfilling the standards') but also to convince the different adults involved in the supervision (class teacher, mentor, tutor) that they are taking their advice seriously and acting upon it. Every trainee learns the importance of maintaining an open dialogue with each significant person in school and demonstrating a willingness to implement their suggestions, so it is essential to keep discussing and sharing insights and concerns with your colleagues.

There are also events that impinge upon the regular teaching programme and affect every person in school. These 'intrusions' include the annual national testing, inspections, interviews for staff vacancies, festivals, anniversaries and extended assemblies that require flexibility and occasionally necessitate a last-minute change of plans. Throughout these occasions, it pays to remain upbeat and take the variations in your stride without complaint.

TO THINK ABOUT

- The reason many people go into teaching is to revisit the joy they experienced when they were learners.

- Aim to become the sort of teacher that you would want for your own children.

Key Quote

Schools should be about providing a sense of hope for all, not achievement for the few. (Anon)

CASE STUDY 1.1

The first week

A trainee teacher, Rachel, wrote in her diary about the first few days on school experience, as follows:

It's the end of the first week of my school placement and I feel quite positive, as actually the week went better than I'd anticipated. I'm doing a lot more teaching than I expected and I have been up quite late planning, sometimes until after midnight. I enjoyed the staff development day about teaching English. I would like to get really organised with the planning so that I'm doing less of it during the working week.

My lessons went fine today. I taught RE which went down surprisingly well and I also told them about the life of children who worked down mines. A lot of the class seemed quite excited about it and generally listened carefully, though there are a few whose attention wandered and I need to work out some way of getting them involved and interested. I must also try to cut down on the content of each lesson because I try to pack too much in, but apart from that things have been going okay. I'm off to write my weekly reflection now and then I must start organising the weekend so that I can get all my planning and preparation fitted into the busy schedule. The teachers in school are warming to me; they seem to be getting much more amenable, if that's the right word, and we're building up a rapport. For the first couple of days I was very anxious about my relationship with the class teacher because she didn't seem to have much time to discuss matters. I appreciate she's got to prepare children for the tests and a lot of things are going on in school but I needed her exclusive attention. Anyway, we seem to be getting much closer now. She's smiling when she talks to me and hopefully everything will be fine. My confidence and enthusiasm are rising fast!

ACTION POINTS ACTION POINTS ACTION POINTS ACTION POINTS ACTION POINTS

> It takes at least a week for most people to settle into a new school situation, so you must be patient and persevere.

> Trainee teachers are strongly influenced by the host teacher's attitude towards them, so it is vital for you to facilitate a good rapport by being personable, responsive and supportive of colleagues.

The complex task of teaching

Developing competence

Very few people seem to be completely natural teachers in the sense of knowing instinctively what to do and how and when to do it. All trainees possess attributes that are useful for the job but also have areas of weakness that require development. Whether they are 'naturals' or 'grafters', trainees have to be willing to listen to advice and hone their classroom practice.

Demonstrating your competence is rooted in good *subject knowledge* and its employment in teaching, *skill acquisition* (e.g. giving clear explanations, use of the whiteboard), *demonstrating professional judgement* influenced by careful reflection on practice (characterised by dozens of daily decisions about what to say, how to behave and when to act), willingness to *draw on and respond to advice* from experienced colleagues and an ability to *work as a team member*. No wonder trainees get tired!

The Training and Development Agency for schools (TDA) has analysed teaching by means of an itemised checklist, in a belief that skills and strategies can be identified, mastered and implemented to create a seamless robe of competence. However, judging teaching effectiveness needs to take account of personal intention, pupil disposition, the intelligent application of knowledge and the interrelatedness of dozens of different decisions that impinge on teacher–pupil interactions. Even when set criteria are used, their *interpretation* requires professional judgement with regard to the prevailing school and classroom priorities that have been established by the host teachers.

While there is a need to take close account of externally imposed targets and the need to maintain academic standards, you must resist the temptation to 'teach to the test'. The best teachers learn to strike a balance between following a predetermined lesson plan and responding to spontaneous opportunities. The more confidence you gain as a teacher, the more willing you become to trust your instincts. Making correct judgements about when to be didactic (teach directly with minimal pupil contribution) and when to promote discovery learning (in which you provide an open-ended task for children to investigate with minimal adult intervention) and when to use a mixture of the two demands sensitivity to the curriculum content, insight into the way that children learn best (Harnett, 2007) and an awareness of time constraints. Sometimes you would like children to explore ideas fully when time factors oblige you to employ more direct teaching methods. However, you can still make the lesson 'come alive' by your enthusiasm, attention to detail and responsiveness to the children's ideas. In fact, the more you involve children in their learning and discuss with them how they learn, the more enthusiastic they become.

One of the attractions of being a teacher is the freedom and flexibility attached to the various roles that teachers are called upon to play. At the same time they have to respond rapidly to specific situations that require them to exercise judgement and act decisively. The best practitioners are constantly alert to unanticipated learning opportunities that emerge during a session and 'mining' them fully. The lesson plan then becomes a guide and not a straitjacket. Richards (2006) helpfully comments:

> *I believe that primary teaching is an extremely complex activity, whether considered in theoretical or practical terms. It's an amalgam of so many elements: interpersonal, intellectual, physical, spiritual, even aesthetic. It changes subtly in form, substance and 'feel' hour to hour, lesson to lesson, class to class, year to year. It involves notions such as 'respect', 'concern', 'care' and 'intellectual integrity' that are impossible to define but which are deeply influential in determining the nature of life in classrooms. (p13)*

Making progress as a teacher

All new teachers take time to adjust and settle into the school and find their feet in the classroom. Trainees who start slowly sometimes accelerate and exceed expectations once they gain confidence. Some trainees who initially make strong headway may fail to achieve their potential, either because they become exhausted with the effort they have made early in the placement or because their initial promise owed more to enthusiasm than to ability.

It is unwise to compare yourself with a fellow student who, in your eyes, seems to be making better progress than you are. Every placement situation is different and makes varied demands on the trainee. Concentrate on the task in hand and don't be unduly distracted by praise or by criticism – just keep learning, persevering, contributing and celebrating.

A characteristic of successful teachers is *professional humility* as they strive to improve their practice while acknowledging their limitations and giving credit to the contribution that colleagues make to their development. Naturally, the attitude of the trainee teacher is a crucial factor in this regard. One trainee teacher might be hardworking, diligent, responsive to advice and impressing the teacher with her or his positive attitude. Another trainee may come across as sullen or lazy or unwilling to face his or her limitations. It is obvious that the first trainee will prosper whereas the second will languish. A minority of talented trainee teachers are reluctant to accept advice in the mistaken belief that they do not have anything more to learn, but such an attitude annoys the host teachers and stifles progress. By contrast, a trainee who shows an eagerness to improve and is willing to confront weaker areas will grow as a professional and gain the admiration and approval of colleagues. Making a determined effort to gain a positive reputation will greatly assist you in your quest for success

While acclimatising to your placement situation it is helpful to remember that the class teacher has to make adjustments in accommodating you in the classroom, not least in relinquishing a degree of control over the class and trusting you to maintain standards in pupil learning. Thankfully, every survey indicates that the large majority of trainee teachers are placed in supportive environments (e.g. Hayes, 2003). It is highly likely that you will find yourself surrounded by sympathetic colleagues and receive clear guidance from the tutor and class teacher, which, together with your own gritty determination, ensures that your time in school is well spent.

In practice the majority of trainees make gradual and cautious progress most of the time, like someone trying to climb carefully an icy slope. They edge forward, only to slip back due to unexpected problems, inexperience in knowing where to place their efforts and the effects of exertion. However, just as suddenly they make an unexpected breakthrough and teaching seems effortless. Your progress as a teacher also resembles a ride on a fairground roller-coaster as opposed to standing on a gently ascending escalator – and far more exciting! If you sometimes feel that your teaching is becoming worse, do not despair; it is because your expectations of yourself have grown.

TO THINK ABOUT
TO THINK ABOUT

Your professional learning does not accumulate on top of existing knowledge like bricks in a wall; rather, it is an active, dynamic process in which ideas and understanding criss-cross and amalgamate.

The teacher's day

Establishing priorities

The primary teacher's day is characterised by busyness and diversity. As a result, the role is complex and difficult to manage in a smooth, predictable and orderly manner. Teachers have to respond to numerous unexpected demands and make rapid decisions about priorities. Such intensity requires a sustained high level of commitment and dedication to the job, which surveys reveal as being present in the vast majority of new teachers (Hayes, 2004). For instance, during break times and after school, teachers commonly choose to undertake work-related tasks or voluntary activities, despite the additional burden it imposes on them.

Although such dedication is commendable, you must also learn to step back from the action and allow your mind and body time to recover. Attempts to import more and more content into the same amount of teaching time while maintaining standards of pupil work and behaviour is a challenge for even the most dedicated teacher. Accepting responsibility for running a club, overseeing a team or assisting with an activity, while valuable experiences, must not be allowed to sap your energy at the expense of lesson preparation, keeping abreast of marking and completing the numerous tasks demanded of you during a school placement. Be wary of telltale signs of fatigue:

- **lack of concentration;**
- **unaccountable irritability;**
- **pessimism regarding the children.**

and take early action to offset their effects. Remember that the school's greatest resource is a fresh, well motivated teacher.

Role diversity

Years ago, primary teachers used to be at liberty to design their own schedules, spending more time on those areas of the curriculum that were deemed to need attention and suspending those that were less pressing. This flexibility had the disadvantage of tempting teachers to concentrate too much on their 'favourite' curriculum areas, but the strong advantage of giving children lots of time to immerse themselves in learning. Today, teachers have relatively little room for manoeuvre about how to allocate teaching time; the mornings are normally used for structured literacy and numeracy sessions as part of a regulated programme of work. The afternoons allow for greater variety, but you will need to work hard to carve out additional time for the completion of important and interesting activities and spontaneous opportunities.

Only slightly more than a half of a primary teacher's professional work is undertaken with pupils in a 'face-to-face' situation. You should not only view your vocation as active teaching but also in terms of staff membership and wider professional engagement. Thus planning and preparation time, marking and assessment of work, supervisory duties, curriculum leadership, staff meetings and contact with parents consume almost as much time as the act of teaching. Social contacts, collaboration with colleagues, harnessing and managing resources, sorting out visits and special events, and perhaps liaising with teachers in other schools also absorb extensive amounts of time for qualified teachers. Such activities require the application of a range of skills and expertise, such as negotiating, organising, speculating and communicating with people inside and outside the school. There's more to being a teacher than teaching.

Improving your work as a teacher

A teacher's role diversity requires that you are alert to the factors that impact upon your effectiveness. In particular, four issues need to be addressed:

- **managing the demands;**
- **distractions and diversions;**
- **time management;**
- **isolation from colleagues.**

Managing the demands

The pace of life sometimes threatens to overwhelm teachers as they endeavour to cope with the job's numerous requirements. The rapidity and speed of events increases the likelihood of flawed judgements or over-hasty responses, so you need to develop the skill of evaluating the significance of demands and how you should deal with them. You must resist becoming submerged by trivial matters that do not necessitate your immediate attention and include short 'time-out' periods for reflection about your schedule. If you are uncertain about priorities, seek advice from the class teacher or tutor.

Distractions and diversions

There are many distractions and diversions from the regular teaching pattern that teachers have to manage during the day, such as resolving pupil disputes, liaising with colleagues and checking equipment. It pays to think ahead and anticipate potential pressure moments, as they can create a swamping effect that can lead to a state of 'action paralysis'. Mentally think through the next session, make sure that you are clear about what you want to achieve, then direct your energies purposefully to that end.

Time management

No matter how many hours are worked, there never seems to be sufficient time to do everything as thoroughly as you wish. Ongoing issues (such as a child's continuing uncooperativeness) or non-completion of tasks (such as marking) often builds up over a week and increases the sense of being overwhelmed. Each delay in task completion increases the likelihood that pressures will accumulate and destabilise the daily rhythm, thus adding to the pressure. A system based on, 'do it now if I possibly can' will alleviate some of these time pressures. For other tasks, divide them into four categories:

- **important and urgent;**
- **important but not urgent;**
- **not important but urgent;**
- **not important and not urgent.**

Deal with important and urgent items first; keep important but not urgent tasks 'ticking over' while you address not important but urgent matters. If something is not important or urgent it can wait its turn!

Isolation from colleagues

Every teacher, however inexperienced, plays a role in maintaining staff harmony and promoting collegiality. Yet even in a school where collaboration and teamwork figure strongly, a large proportion of the teacher's role involves physical separation from other adults. It pays to establish and maintain comradeship despite the intensity of business that each day brings. Joyful teaching is the right of every teacher and is greatly assisted by your supportive and sensitive attitude towards colleagues and good communication skills.

CASE STUDY 1.2

My teacher

A trainee teacher, Ava, reflected on her own experiences as a pupil.

At the age of nine my family moved from an inner-city to a rural area to live. My experience of school had been very negative up until then. I was regarded as very low ability in all subjects and although I had friends I didn't enjoy school at all. My first day in my new junior school arrived. It was just after the Easter break and I was dreading being 'the new girl'. I walked into the room and there in front of me was the kindest face with the biggest warm smile I had ever seen. My new teacher was the best thing that ever happened in my schooling. She gave me confidence and enthusiasm for learning. My ability in all subjects seemed to rise effortlessly and I enjoyed going to school.

As I grew older I decided that I had been looking at my old teacher through rose-tinted glasses, so when the opportunity arose to gain work experience in her classroom I jumped at the chance. Watching her teaching and seeing her good relationship with the children made me realise that she was just as good as I remembered. I had already decided that I wished to become a teacher, but this is when I first realised what kind of teacher I wished to be.

ACTION POINTS ACTION POINTS ACTION POINTS ACTION POINTS ACTION POINTS

> **Feed and exercise children's imaginations by use of story, poetry, drama and heightening the sense of mystery in learning.**

> **Anticipate children asking you why they are doing the activity and have a good answer ready.**

> **Convince children that they can succeed by their own perseverance and with your help.**

> **Avoid covering a lot of curriculum territory superficially; instead, foster deep learning and reinforce it at every opportunity.**

Key Quote
All effective teachers have a passion for their subject, a passion for their pupils and a passionate belief that who they are and how they teach can make a difference in their pupils' lives, both in the moment of teaching and in the days, weeks, months and even years afterwards. (Day, 2004, p12)

Conclusion

Joyful teaching does not happen by chance. It blossoms where pupils and adult enthusiastically engage with learning, relish challenges, and keep success and failure in perspective. There are at least four strategies to employ in gaining the most from your work as a teacher.

1. *Persevere to stay positive*. For trainee teachers the greatest enemy is fear of failure, despite the fact that the vast majority of trainees on placement are successful. Every teaching experience has its share of ups and downs; these experiences indicate that professional learning is taking place and should not be viewed as indicators of your inadequacy.
2. *View teaching as an adventure*. Reflect on your strengths and weaknesses but avoid brooding over shortcomings. Teaching is a thrilling occupation but like any complex job it takes time to develop and mature. Treat setbacks as slip-ups that will pitch you forward rather than downwards! Train yourself to smile at minor errors and act to correct them instead of brooding over them miserably.

3. *Refuse to adopt a victim mentality*. Make sure you keep fully abreast of the training and assessment process and the way it impacts upon your progress and attainment. If you find yourself waking anxiously in the early hours, take immediate action. Write down the nature of your concerns and pursue the matter until it is resolved satisfactorily and you experience peace of mind.

4. *Practise your teaching skills diligently*. As with a craftsperson or performer, teaching involves considerable artistry, so mull over the strategies and approaches you employ with as much attention as a surgeon would do prior to undertaking a major operation. Rehearse and practise the way you speak, explain facts and ask questions. In aspiring to achieve high standards, however, be reassured that unlike a surgeon, the patient will live if you make a mistake!

Finally, despite the demands and high level of commitment required in teaching, it is one of the most rewarding careers imaginable. The knowledge that you are helping to shape and mould the next generation should inspire you and bring joy to your heart (Manuel, 2006).

Further reading

Hayes, D. (2006) *Inspiring Primary Teaching*. Exeter: Learning Matters.
The author puts passion for learning at the heart of excellent teaching.

Liston, D. and Garrison, J. (2004) *Teaching, Learning and Loving*. Abingdon: Routledge.
The book emphasises the importance of emotion in teaching and learning.

Medwell, J. (2007) *Successful Teaching Placement: Primary and Early Years*. Exeter: Learning Matters.
The book provides a practical guide to school experience for trainee teachers.

References

Day, C. (2004) *Passion for Teaching*. Abingdon: Routledge.
Harnett, P. (2007) *Supporting Children's Learning in the Primary and Early Years*. Abingdon: Routledge.
Hayes, D. (2003) Emotional preparation for teaching: a case study about trainee teachers in England. *Journal of Teacher Development*, 7 (2), 153–71.
Hayes, D. (2004) Recruitment and retention: insights into the motivation of primary trainee teachers in England. *Research in Education*, 71, 37–49.
Manuel, J. (2006) It has always been my dream: exploring pre-service teachers' motivations for choosing to teach. *Teacher Development*, 10 (1), 5–24.
Richards, C. (2006) Primary teaching: a personal perspective, in J. Arthur, T. Grainger and D. Wray (eds) *Learning to Teach in the Primary School*. Abingdon: Routledge, pp11–21.

2
The joy of enhancing children's learning

Peter Kelly

Introduction

In this chapter I suggest that learning happens everywhere, often without us even noticing, but when we focus on learning it can make it more difficult to achieve. This means that some of the things we do in schools get in the way of learning. I argue, however, that we can improve school learning by including opportunities for learning which are more like those out of school, and in the second part of the chapter I describe such opportunities, these being the basis of an enhanced curriculum.

Ubiquitous learning

Think about the things you have already done today – perhaps you have made yourself some breakfast or lunch, read a newspaper or watched the television news, sent a text or e-mailed a friend, driven or cycled to college or university. Some of you might have been for a swim or gone to the gym. Where did you learn to do these things – at school, in formal lessons, by watching others or did you teach yourself? The answer is probably a mixture of each of these and through many other ways as well.

The fascinating thing is that learning is happening for each of us, all of the time, and much of the time we don't even think about it. When I watch the news on television I am learning about the world, and I make sense of the world I see through the medium of television news by referring to lots of other experiences – whether I watched the news yesterday, whether I've been to the places reported on, how much I know about those places or the background to the events described, and so on. Watching the news is a learning experience. So is travelling and cooking. Think of the last time you really enjoyed reading a book, or watched a documentary with interest, or enjoyed a film at the cinema, or travelled somewhere new and immersed yourself in a different culture. Think of your hobbies and interests. Think about reading a newspaper or voting in the last general election. It is hard to think of an event in adult life that isn't learned and doesn't bring about new learning when you engage in it. When I cook a meal I am helped by the many experiences of cooking that I have already had, and once I have finished that experience becomes one to refer to next time I cook. But for the most part we don't notice the learning because we are preoccupied with the doing – whether that is making a meal, enjoying the film or book, or building the new fence.

Learning is ubiquitous – it goes on everywhere, is as much a natural process as breathing, and for the most part in our everyday lives we take it for granted. Yet we tend to associate the idea of learning with particular places, those where formal learning takes place – schools, colleges, universities and the like.

Intuitive learning

For most of us for most of the time the learning is intuitive, a process which we are seldom aware of. We only become conscious of it when we are asked to focus on it, but otherwise it hums away in the background as we get on with doing other things. In this respect learning is just like breathing. When I walk down the road or go about my usual daily business I don't think about my breathing even though it continues successfully, so allowing me to get things done. Occasionally it helps if I focus on my breathing, perhaps while swimming or running, that is, when I am exerting myself in some way. But as I become an expert swimmer or runner, or as I become fitter, I will probably focus far less on my breathing again. Of course some people will be aware of their breathing more often than others, and some will need special help to facilitate their breathing – be it long-term such as that required by those with asthma or short-term for those with, say, a chest infection.

I've probably exhausted this analogy, but I hope you get the idea. Learning is a natural process – most of the time people just get on with it, they aren't even aware of it happening. Nevertheless there are times when it is useful to focus on it, and from time to time we all need help with learning – be it long-term or short-term. Some have difficulties learning specific things – and of course, as with any natural process, some have difficulties preventing their success in much broader terms. But, when asked about hobbies, interests and out-of-school achievements, most if not all learners can describe some things which they have learnt successfully.

CASE STUDY 2.1

Expert knowledge

I have a favourite story about a child I once taught which illustrates this. I'm sure you'll be able to think of similar children from your own experiences. Many years ago I was a primary school teacher. One lunchtime I had had to nip out of school to visit the bank, and as I drove back onto the school site I could see a nine-year-old boy who was in my class watching me from the corner of the school field nearest to the car park.

After lunch he came into class and told me that he had heard my car engine misfire as I accelerated away from school at the start of lunch, but that it seemed okay when I drove slowly into the car park on my return. He went on to tell me that there were a number of things which could be wrong with my car. As the car was misfiring when cold it could be that my spark plugs might need replacing. However, the engine started easily, which he wouldn't expect if the plugs were at fault. He then said that it could be a fuel problem, but most misfiring problems were in fact electrical. Finally he concluded that it was most likely that the fault lay with the ignition wires or distributor and that I should get these checked. Sure enough, when I visited a garage later that day I was told that the ignition wires did indeed need replacing as there was a short circuit from one of them.

What made my earlier conversation all the more interesting was that this boy could read at the level of a six-year-old and write very little indeed, apart from his name. He had significant learning difficulties when it came to these, yet he could express himself so clearly in the area of 'engine troubleshooting'. Further, he could consider the solution to a problem from a number of perspectives, using evidence to make inferences based on his knowledge of how an engine works. This had been learned while helping his father who owned a local garage but who spent a good deal of his spare time working on cars at his home. The knowledge he had gained from this apprenticeship with his father had taken him towards becoming an expert problem solver in car mechanics – at nine years of age!

Research has supported the conclusion that children can and often do engage in extremely sophisticated thinking. For example, in one well known study by Terezinha Nunes and her colleagues in the 1980s, the mathematical competences of Brazilian street children were examined (Nunes, 1993). These children were street traders who had to purchase goods from various wholesalers, price the goods and then sell them. The mathematics involved was complex, especially as Brazil's rate of inflation at the time was 250 per cent per annum – and had to be accounted for by the children. The children, only one of whom had been at formal school for more than four years, were observed to achieve a 98 per cent overall success rate in making these extremely complex calculations in their day-to-day trading activities. Interestingly the study also found that the children were unable to use these mathematical competences when taken into an academic environment: their ability to do these calculations depended on the context in which they were needed and which gave them meaning.

School learning

ACTION POINTS ACTION POINTS ACTION POINTS ACTION POINTS ACTION POINTS

When you are next in a primary school, choose a small group of children, whatever age – although younger children may offer more interesting answers – and ask them why they think they learn, say, mathematics. If I were a betting man I'd put money on the following answers being among the most common responses, especially with older children:

> to get better at maths;

> to help me when I am doing maths later on;

> to help me pass tests;

> to help me when I get to secondary school.

Try it and find out!

Assuming I am right, why might this be? First, assessment has a huge effect on children's learning, something I will return to in a later chapter. The testing stakes are high for children. Pressure is put on them by schools through the use of extra classes to 'boost' their performance, revision materials, homework, teaching that continually asserts the importance of tests and so on. Indeed, in England the national testing experience at the end of Year 6 has become a ritual rite of passage for many 11-year-olds at the culmination of their primary schooling. It is inevitable that children will notice the importance placed upon tests and that this will influence their views of learning.

Second, most learning in school is formalised, that is it is stripped of the context that makes it meaningful. Let's look at mathematics again. The original version of the National Numeracy Strategy describes numeracy as 'a key life skill', and adds that without basic numeracy skills, our children will be disadvantaged throughout life (DfEE, 1999). The word 'skill' is important because it implies that such mathematical learning can be unproblematically transferred from one context – the context of learning – to another – the context of application. But much mathematics teaching in English primary schools attempts simply to develop children's ability to carry out calculations involving number in a variety of almost entirely schooling contexts as measured almost entirely through national tests. Rarely are contexts from everyday life or methods of appraising children's performance other than testing included. Little wonder that our children find the use and application of mathematics so difficult.

It is therefore not surprising when, no matter how well we teach subjects such as mathematics, children see most of their learning as being of little value to them beyond school success or testing, and thus remain unable or reluctant to use their learning outside school. Being tied so closely to 'performance' in school, their knowledge becomes largely inert away from school.

Many factors influence the learner's experience of and engagement with their learning, and although little research has focused on primary aged children, the findings of studies of older learners illuminate some of the influences younger learners face. Not only overbearing assessment systems which emphasise testing, but also highly intensive and fast-moving courses, content-filled curricula and an overuse of traditional instruction-led teaching methods have all been linked strongly with the adoption by learners of surface approaches to learning. As this list encompasses the kind of regimes which decades of initiatives have encouraged in our primary schools, it is no surprise that so many children in them do not think about or engage with their learning.

Out-of-school learning

Out of school, people tend to focus on doing things which they need to do or which interest them rather than learning. So, one child might spend a weekend pottering about in their garden, making dens, sweeping up leaves and the like, while another spends the same time playing football at the local park or practising moves on their bike or skateboard. A third could be absorbed for a whole afternoon making a house from a commercial construction kit, while another spends the same time engaged in role play, revisiting stories from a book that he or she has read. Each of these activities brings about learning – whether about gardening and nature, buildings and structures, roles and relationships, or indeed many other possibilities. Despite not being the focus of our attention, such everyday learning is very effective and we can draw lessons from this in striving to improve school learning. Analysing everyday learning evokes three important principles: (1) learning is a by-product of our engagement in other activities; (2) it is relevant to the things we want to do and achieve; (3) it is often interest driven.

Often children occupied in out-of-school activities do so for some considerable time, without interruption, sometimes returning to them again and again until they are finished – think of the den builder, the skateboarder or the role player. In such cases they are self-directed, have complete ownership of what they are doing, and as a result become deeply engaged in their activities. To some extent they are autonomous learners: making choices depending on what interests them, what they want to achieve and what they think they need to do in order to achieve this, all in relation to the things they know they can already do, the resources they have available to them and their previous experiences of doing similar things.

Of course, out-of-school learning can be formalised – think of music lessons, drama societies or sporting clubs. But even so, children often choose to attend these, so their participation is interest driven and their work is focused on doing the activity and on performance rather than on meeting learning intentions.

Enhancing learning

By comparing learning in school with learning out of school, we can draw up a list of suggestions for the kind of work we could provide for our children to enhance their experience of learning in school. Each of the following suggestions is linked and the order in which they are listed is not meant to indicate their relative importance.

Help children make sense of the world

We should at all times try to make children's activities in school meaningful to them, and in so doing, to help them make sense of their world and help them understand how others have made sense of it. Whether this is the sense they make of how the world works (science), of how people lived long ago (history) or of how people live in other parts of the world (geography), or whether it is the sense they make of the world through speaking, listening, reading, writing or mathematics, all children's learning in school should focus on helping them better understand the world in which they live.

Local relevance

To be meaningful, the activities we plan at school should draw and build on the day-to-day experiences of the children themselves – and that often means making use of local examples, resources, opportunities, interests, issues and concerns, and so on. Inviting local authors or artists into school to talk about their work, exploring local history and using local examples which the children may well know of as a basis for geography are all aspects of good practice. Think about the locality in which the school is situated. What is nearby? Are there any landmarks, well known features or traditions? What are its predominant characteristics? And, in considering your answers, what opportunities do these provide for making children's learning link to their everyday experiences?

Respond to current interests and events

Everyday learning is driven by need and interest. School learning can be the same if it is opportunistic – if it makes the most of school events, community events and even national events to capture children's enthusiasm. So, whether it is a national or international sporting event such as football's World Cup or the Olympic Games, whether it is a community anniversary or festival, or whether it is a school event like a play or concert, each can be harnessed for learning. So can unplanned events: the first fall of snow, a water main problem in town, a storm which makes national news or widely reported events in another part of the world. All these events provide opportunities for discussion, activity and learning, and we need to be flexible to make the most of such opportunities.

Relate to current and immediate experience

Many things happen in children's lives both in and out of school, but school life seems to trundle on, unstoppable, often without reference to or acknowledgement of these. The birth of a brother or sister, an upsetting event in the playground, a recent or anticipated holiday, success in a weekend sporting event, the death of an elderly grandparent, all are important events to some children in the class and can provide learning opportunities for all. By utilising such opportunities we show children that school work is of relevance to their everyday lives and that they are more than a cog in the machine of school. By so valuing children, we can help increase their ownership of school learning.

Relate to previous experiences

Learning is also about making links, and we have discussed linking school learning to the locality in which the school is situated and to current events and experiences. We must also help children make links with their previous experiences. When we introduce something new we might ask what they already know about it, whether they remember looking at it before, whether it links to anything they know of or have done out of school, and so on. We might also help them make links within and across subjects. For example, when we evaluate children's performances in gymnastics, we might talk of the questions we asked when evaluating our models in Technology and if the same questions would be helpful for PE.

Experiential

Meaningful learning should, first and foremost, be first-hand, not passively received through the descriptions of a teacher, the lens of a television camera or the words on a page or computer screen. Children learn best through active engagement and direct experience: it is better to explore fabrics and materials and feel their properties than to be told about them; it makes more sense when you act out the drama of Saxon village life or experience at first-hand a real Saxon pot than when you look at pictures of these; and so on. Of course children will always need to spend some of their time learning from listening, watching or reading – indeed these are worthwhile and valuable activities when learners engage in them actively. It is by drawing on a rich and full range of direct experiences and reflecting on these that children are able to become active listeners, watchers or readers.

Develop awe and wonder

Finally, in all of the above we must strive to capture children's imaginations, to provide them with sparks of excitement and enthuse them with glimpses of what the world has to offer. Only then will we encourage them to have a passion for learning and so become lifelong learners.

For children to work in such ways and to encourage quality in their work it is important we allow them extended uninterrupted time in which to do so, thereby encouraging a deeper engagement with their work. It is also important that children are allowed to make choices, but being able to make a choice involves having a range of options available to you. So, not being able to use a pair of scissors, hold a pencil, use a paintbrush and so on will limit the range of possible ways you can respond to a task. Further, not being able to read, spell, write in a variety of genres, present ideas orally to a group or work collaboratively will also be limiting. Finally, one may have the skills but not the resources. Thus the provision of a range of resources of appropriate quality which the children know how to use and care for and from which they can select is important.

TO THINK ABOUT

The tasks we provide for our children should:

- **help them make sense of the world;**
- **be locally relevant;**
- **respond to their current interests and events;**
- **relate to their current and immediate experience;**
- **relate to their previous experiences;**
- **be experiential;**
- **develop awe and wonder.**

Conclusion

Formal learning in school is, for many children, separate from and irrelevant to their everyday lives. At worst this renders school learning inert – useless beyond the context of school. Everyday learning is ubiquitous, intuitive, useful and fun. The contrast is stark, but if we want to encourage today's children to be lifelong learners it is a disparity we must address. One way of beginning to do so is to acknowledge the value of children's everyday learning and make classroom learning more like this.

ACTION POINTS ACTION POINTS ACTION POINTS ACTION POINTS ACTION POINTS

To develop quality you should:

> allow children extended uninterrupted time on tasks;

> allow children time and opportunities to make choices;

> teach children the skills to enable them to work autonomously;

> provide a range of appropriate quality resources for children to choose from, and teach them how to use these appropriately.

Further reading

Bobbit-Nolan, S. (1995) Teaching for autonomous learning, in C. Desforges (ed.) *An Introduction to Teaching: Psychological Perspectives*. Oxford: Blackwell.
Offers more information on promoting autonomous learning.

Kelly, P. (2005) *Using Thinking Skills in the Primary Classroom*. London: Sage.
Provides a more detailed consideration of social learning and apprenticeship approaches, together with a wide range of examples and many suggestions for enhancing practice.

References

DfEE (1999) *The National Numeracy Strategy: Framework for Teaching Mathematics from Reception to Year 6*. London: DfEE.
Nunes, T., Schliemann, A. and Carraher, D. (1993) *Street Mathematics and School Mathematics*. Cambridge: Cambridge University Press.

3
Thinking together: enjoying dialogue with children

Joanna Haynes

Introduction

Most young children are driven to explore the world around them and they constantly ask all kinds of questions. These questions can be very probing and philosophical in flavour: *Am I real? Where was I before I was born? Why can't ladies be dads? How do you know when you're dreaming? Can something be sad and beautiful at the same time?* Adults are variously fascinated, amused and driven mad by children's boundless curiosity and desire to keep asking, why? It is often these qualities of openness and enthusiasm in children that attract people into primary teaching. Children's eagerness seems to create an inviting space of discovery and possibility.

As well as being curious, children frame their questions in a fresh and direct way, providing a wonderful opportunity to converse about the meaning of words. Questions like: *How do things get into your mind? Is there a plug at the bottom of the sea? How do cats kiss? Is the sky all joined together? What if heaven is full?* prompt us to reconsider ideas or to doubt beliefs and perceptions that we have come to take for granted. Conversation is enriched when adults are willing to join in with children's perplexity and searching. With some encouragement from those around them, questioning is a way in which children demonstrate their capacity to initiate and pursue their own day-to-day education. What is significant for those with an interest in effective teaching is the way in which much of this early learning takes place through everyday conversation.

Classroom interaction

Questioning, reasoning and dialogue

Talking is a fundamental form of expression for each individual located 'between' persons as conversation. It is the basic vehicle for personal engagement with others and serves to develop thought and identity. This implies that educational practice in speaking and listening should support and give opportunity for talk and opportunity to listen in ways that are authentic rather than contrived. Each speech event relates to the particularity in which it is embedded; the objective of class-room talk should enable speakers to become perceptive listeners, interpreters and versatile participants rather than to be programmed. (Doddington, 2001, p273)

The classroom is a very different kind of learning context from the worlds that children have experienced before they come to school. In schools pupils talk far less and much more rarely initiate the kind of verbal interaction that leads to deep intellectual quests for understanding. In the classroom teachers are in charge and most verbal interaction is planned and initiated by them. Teachers know how important questions are but, even when they encourage questioning and keep a careful log of questions asked, they can be disappointed by both the quantity and quality of pupil questioning and the resulting interaction. The vast majority of teachers' questions, perhaps necessarily, are 'closed', i.e. they already know the answer and they are 'fishing' to check whether pupils do as well. While this kind of questioning is an essential part of the teaching repertoire, if it happens too frequently or is the only type of teacher–pupil interaction that takes place, children can quickly learn that there is usually only one 'right answer' to a question.

As seen from some of the children's questions mentioned already, not all questions have a single answer and vast areas of human knowledge are much more uncertain and provisional. When it comes to these deeper questions about the world or how we live, a distinctive kind of interaction is valuable in helping to create meaning and in encouraging deeper thinking and independent reasoning. We need to thoughtfully cultivate the kind of teaching space where conversation is kept open and where everyone feels confident and free to explore ideas in progress. This is all very well in spontaneous interaction between adults and children, but how can these qualities of learning be nurtured in the more formal and organised setting of the primary classroom? How can we generate the kind of activity of minds sometimes referred to as 'higher order' thinking and interaction (Fisher, 1990)? Children describe it as the kind of thinking that makes their minds burst or their brains hurt.

Philosophy for Children is a distinctive approach to teaching that promotes questioning, reasoning and dialogue (Lipman, 1991; 1993). It offers a means to build on the searching characteristics young learners display *within* the context and structure of the primary curriculum. Using and developing *Philosophy for Children* has had a big impact on my teaching as well as the way I think about children as learners. It has made me listen much more attentively. It is possible to create a mood of enquiry in which children are more likely to ask probing questions and the remainder of this chapter provides both examples and practical suggestions to illustrate ways in which such questions can be pursued through collaborative dialogue (Murris and Haynes, 2000; Haynes, 2002).

An educational viewpoint to consider:

- a class is a *community* made up of individuals;
- children's *voices* need to be heard and to learn effectively they need to be able to *participate* meaningfully in their class community;
- adults have to work at *listening* and *responding* to children's voices;
- it is important to make proper time and space for *dialogue* in the classroom.

The art of questioning in the classroom

While most primary schools work with a common curriculum, every school is made up of individuals trying to interpret and make sense and meaning of the world through their experience and by talking with one another. In a rapidly changing world a person's ability to think and solve problems, to reason and collaborate, is vital. Many curricula reflect this view and advise active teaching of critical and creative thinking, reasoning and a wide range of information processing and communication skills. These capacities are regarded as valuable in employment, in family and community life and in enabling people both to belong to and to participate in the wider society.

There is a growing interest in methods of teaching that strengthen pupils' listening, speaking and thinking and that promote independence of mind and spirit, along with the ability to work well with others. These methods often require the teacher to stop being the 'font of knowledge' delivering ideas and to be more of a facilitator of learning. This is a demanding role that emphasises listening, challenging children's thinking and deepening classroom dialogue.

The Greek philosopher Socrates suggested that to encourage thinking in others is to adopt the role of a midwife, helping others to 'give birth' to their ideas. To assist with this birthing process, at the heart of the philosophical approach to teaching is the art of questioning. Philosophy is concerned with the kind of questions that do not have firm answers and that we can answer only through reasoning and deliberation with each other. In supporting children's dialogue with one another and helping them to build on each other's ideas, the philosophical teacher uses certain types of question to deepen and extend an enquiry that begins from a child's comment or question.

Thinking about teachers' questions

Open procedural questions are not content specific but help to encourage further thinking and understanding. For example:

- **Could you give a reason for what you are saying?**

- **Is there a connection between your idea and Susan's?**

- **Can you think of an example?**

- **Is x the same as y or is it different?**

- **Do you agree or disagree with Ahmed?**

- **Has anyone changed their mind after hearing Chantal?**

Open substantive questions focus on content of ideas and draw attention to core philosophical/ abstract concepts being discussed. For example:

- **Does time have a *beginning*?**

- **What do you mean by saying the princess was *in love*?**

- **What makes you think the robber was *bad*?**

- **What if there were *no rules*?**

As well as paying attention to her own questioning, a teacher who adopts this style of facilitation will encourage children to give careful consideration to the nature and framing of their own questions, too.

Thinking about children's questions:

Sara Stanley (2004) uses the following categories to help her reception class analyse questions:

- *Closed questions* – with a clear and obvious answer not requiring discussion (marked by a tick symbol), for example:
  - Did the bear eat the porridge?
  - How many chairs were there?

- *Factual questions* – you can ask someone or look it up (marked by symbol of a book)
  - How did the wolf get down the chimney?
  - What was the cat's name?

- *Open-ended questions* – invite expression of opinions and interpretation (marked by smiley face symbol), for example:
  - Why was Jack scared of the giant?
  - Why didn't the step-sisters like Cinderella?
- *Philosophical questions* – touch on deep ideas and prompt 'hard thinking' (marked by a large bold question mark symbol), for example:
  - Where do dreams come from?
  - What is love?
  - Is magic true?

Children love sorting questions out and come up with their own unique groupings (questions with no answer, questions with five words, questions you can look up in a book, questions with why, questions about the cat).

Categories can often spill over. This activity helps them to generate criteria, a demanding activity in its own right. Whatever labels you choose, asking questions about questions leads to deep exploration and dialogue.

Stimulating and motivating children in the classroom

Before we get as far as responding to children's questions we have to take certain steps to create situations in which it is more likely that children will be motivated and able to ask them in the first place. One of the most important judgements teachers make on a daily basis is the choice of resources to use for teaching. Whenever we make this selection, we influence the kind of learning interaction that is likely to take place. If we want searching conversations to take place, we have to avoid those resources that seem to tell us exactly what to think and to choose starting points that are genuinely thought-provoking. Luckily, there is plenty of this kind of material around. We might want to begin from a work of art or music, a photograph, a poem, a cartoon or a real-life event. One of the most accessible places to find material that stimulates deeper questioning is in high-quality children's literature, particularly picture books.

There are practical, educational reasons why pictures and picture books are so suited to encouraging questioning and to teaching thinking. Pictorial material offers easier access to ideas for a greater number of children – ideal for young readers or children with reading problems. Picture books can be funny and imaginative, and they are short, entire stories that can be managed in a single lesson slot. A good selection of picture books can include a wide variety of aesthetic styles and cultures, offering children a rich source of ideas. The aesthetic quality of the book enhances the power with which ideas are conveyed – the better a book is illustrated, the more thoughts, feelings and images the reader can work with. The best picture books can be used with any age group to generate stirring and memorable conversations.

Case studies

What follows are some accounts of dialogue among children of different ages in primary school classrooms, stimulated by high-quality picture books and by an invitation from the teacher to comment on the things they find surprising, puzzling or thought-provoking. What the books have in common is that they communicate to young readers that they are taken seriously as thinkers by offering rich, complex and ambiguous pictures and text. It is material that not only leaves room for the reader/viewer, but seems to invite interpretation and tap into deeper wells of experience, thought and feeling.

CASE STUDY 3.1

How did the bird die?

The picture book *Frog and the Birdsong* (Velthuijs, 1991) tells the story of a group of animals who come across a blackbird lying still on the ground. They are not sure what is wrong but eventually decide the bird is dead. They bury it, putting flowers on the grave. On the way home they play happily together and the last illustration shows a tree with a bird in it while the text reads: *There in a tree was a blackbird singing a lovely song – as always*.

Having looked at the book together, the teacher asks the class of six-year-olds to think about what interests them in the story and to explore their ideas through drawing and/or writing. Children work in different parts of the room: some at tables, others on the floor. They whisper from time to time but mostly they are quiet and busy with their own thoughts. Some fill a whole page with ideas and others write just a single question such as *How did the bird die?* The children gather together to talk about their questions and the teacher writes these up for all to see. Amy says, *How do they know the bird died?* and Beth comments, *I think the bird on the tree was the one in the hole*. The class gets stuck into discussion about how the animals could tell whether the bird was really dead. (See Figure 3.1.)

Figure 3.1 Drawing of a blackbird

The teacher writes their suggestions up and they debate each one: *the eyes were open*, *you can check the heartbeat*, *doctors can make your heart start again*. A web of possibilities develops on the whiteboard but the discussion is inconclusive: declaring somebody dead is a complex matter. As they talk, the children purposefully refer to details in the pictures and in the text to confirm or refute ideas. The time for break arrives and the children leave the classroom, still talking about the bird.

CASE STUDY 3.2

What's under the rug?

Questions can lead in surprising directions. What looks at first like a closed or factual question can turn out to be an open one when the thinking behind the question is probed. *The Mysteries of Harris Burdick* (Van Allsberg, 1984) contains a series of black and white images accompanied only by a title and a caption. A class of ten- and eleven-year-olds are working with one image of a man in a living room holding a wooden chair up in the air as he looks down at a large lump under the rug (the caption reads: *Two weeks passed and it happened again*). In small groups children refine and prioritise questions. (See Figure 3.2.)

Each group must choose one question to put forward. In the end the class vote *What is under the rug?* as the question they are keenest to pursue. As they put forward possible answers (*an animal, a ghost, the wind*) one pupil draws everyone's attention to the expression and physical attitude of the man in the picture. What can it mean? Perhaps the man is mad, drunk, on drugs, hallucinating. It moves from a discussion of how to interpret the man in the picture to a more general enquiry. How do we arrive at judgements about the behaviour of others? How do we know whether our judgements are true? Returning to the example of the man in the picture, the teacher asks pupils to define what they mean by 'mad' and they search for examples. A 'concept line' is drawn on the board, with the label 'not mad/normal' at one end and 'mad/not normal' at the other. Pupils engage in lively debate about where to put examples of 'mad' or 'normal' behaviour along the concept line and the teacher acts as scribe, checking carefully that she has understood each child's contribution. The diagrammatic representation seems to sharpen their thinking. As the discussion continues, the mood becomes more tentative. The last pupil to speak suggests, *I don't think anybody is completely mad or completely normal*.

Figure 3.2 One pupil's list of questions prompted by Van Allsberg's picture

CASE STUDY 3.3

Is the night shimmy real or not real?

The Night Shimmy (Strauss and Browne, 1993) is a wonderful picture book for prompting all kinds of enquiry. The main character, Eric, is not too keen on talking. He has a 'friend', the Night Shimmy, who speaks for him and protects him from frightening things that appear in his dreams. Having chosen the question *Was the night shimmy real or not real?* children aged 7–8 years old work in groups, with one person acting as scribe. They are asked to consider arguments for and against the Night Shimmy being real. The teacher suggests that they might organise their ideas under three headings. Their answers are shown in Table 3.1.

Table 3.1 Organising children's ideas

Night Shimmy is real because ...	Night Shimmy is not real because ...	Not sure/other thoughts ...
It might be somebody helping him	It's not real because it's a story book	It might be a ghost

He might be real in Eric's mind	Not real because nobody else can see him	It's a dream, but what kind?
He talks	Fiction book	Ghost or imaginary friend
He is real to Eric	Nobody can fly	
Real to Eric in his imagination	It's just a saying	
Real to Eric because he needs a friend	Things can't disappear	

After the work in small groups, the dialogue moves on again to the question of how to determine whether something is real. Children are clamouring to offer answers: things you can see, things you can touch, things in photographs or on the television. Each time someone puts forward an idea the teacher gently pushes their thinking with a question or faithfully repeats what they have suggested. Soon the teacher is saying little as dialogue flows among the class and children question the truth of each other's examples of what can be known for certain.

CASE STUDY 3.4

Am I dreaming?

Responding to Maurice Sendak's well-known tale *Where the Wild Things Are* (1992), four-, five- and six-year-olds from a mixed infant class ask:

How did Max's bedroom turn into a forest?

How did the monsters get into his bedroom?

Was he sleepwalking?

Was Max dreaming?

Was it Max's imagination?

Were the monsters real?

Was Max wild because he had that suit on?

How come his dinner was still hot when he had been away a long time?

The children draw pictures and talk together with their neighbours on the floor as they explore their ideas (for example, see Figure 3.3). They move into a circle to share their questions, which the teacher has recorded for all to see.

Next time they meet for a session of philosophy they read the story again. Several copies of the book are made available. Some children can read some of the text while others listen and look at the pictures. The children revisit their questions and again there is some reading and some listening. A discussion about dreaming develops. David says, *I think we're dreaming about doing work*. Linda disagrees, *I don't think we're dreaming because the juniors are here*. Natalie adds, *We're not dreaming because we didn't go to sleep first*. This view is confirmed by Robert, *We only have dreams when we're at home in bed*. The teacher listens carefully and encourages everyone to say what they think about dreaming.

Figure 3.3 Dani's drawings and questions

A few days later one of the five-year-olds in the class remarks to the teacher, *Maybe I'm dreaming now, maybe we're all dreaming, maybe everyone in the whole world is dreaming, maybe we won't wake up*. Lines of enquiry that start in a session of philosophical dialogue often remain 'live' for several days or weeks and spill over into other classroom conversations or beyond.

TO THINK ABOUT
TO THINK ABOUT

One of the powerful features of this approach is that adults too are drawn into the philosophical discussion. Some teachers report that parents get involved in these conversations too and Sara Stanley (2004) has developed the idea of thinking journals which children use to share questions and ideas with their teacher and their parents.

Where stories are well chosen they should not appeal only to children but to adults too. This is because they express familiar but unresolved aspects of the human condition and because they are sufficiently ambiguous and complex to invite speculation from the reader or listener. The picture book, *Where the Wild Things Are*, tends to evoke a very strong response from everyone. Some people find it mysterious and amusing, others find it fearful. The book's themes include good and evil, anger and love, time, dreaming and imagination, among others. Adults have asked questions like: Why do we want to eat those we love? Did Max deserve to be punished? How should we express our wild side?

CASE STUDY 3.5

What is naughty?

Tony Bradman's story of Michael, humorously illustrated by Tony Ross (1990), relates the story of a boy who does not fit into school, persistently refuses to conform and gets on with his own thing in spite of being written off by his teachers. At the end of the story he flies off in a rocket that he has constructed from recycled parts, after extensive independent research. The teachers then claim that they 'always knew he would go far'. The children asked questions such as: *How has Michael learned to make a rocket when he hasn't listened in lessons? Should children be able to learn what they want?*

In their discussion the children (ages 7–11) reflect on some of the issues.

James: *He is not actually being naughty when he is reading about rockets. It's just he's learning about something different to what everybody else is doing. He is learning about rockets instead of learning what everyone else is learning.*

Kylie: *I think I know what James' thought means, I think he means that when like Mike whatever his name is, when grows up that he might build a real rocket, as he makes all these play ones.*

Tamsin: *I agree with Kylie because, just 'cos you are not interested in school and what they are learning in school it doesn't mean that out of school you can't learn about something you want to learn about.*

Jane: *He was naughty in a way, but he wasn't. He was naughty for not listening to what the teacher was saying and learning, but he wasn't being naughty by learning his own thing about rockets.*

Stacey: *I agree with Tamsin because he is learning and he isn't learning; he is not doing what the teacher wants him to do, he is doing what he wants to do, but he is still sort of learning about rockets, instead of about maths or science or whatever.*

Laura: *You could hardly call him all naughty because instead of playing football and everything at playtime he learnt on his own, like he was reading instead of playing football.*

Kylie: *I agree with Laura because in some ways they should be happy because he is learning, like he is learning how to read, but he is not reading the books that are in school, he is reading his own kind of thing.*

Supporting children's participation in classroom enquiry and dialogue

In the approach called *Philosophy for Children*, the classroom is set up and the dialogue managed through a process called 'community of enquiry'. Young thinkers can flourish because the medium is mainly oral. Pupils create the agenda for enquiry and there is time to think. There are no 'right answers' and all ideas are given a fair hearing. Support is given to minority points of view. Disagreement is normalised and there is freedom to change one's mind. The teacher is not the 'ultimate authority'. The process of enquiry is flexible and cyclical, a framework rather than a blueprint, as expressed in Table 3.2.

Table 3.2 The process of learning through a community of enquiry

The phases of work in a community of enquiry	Learning opportunities, skills and values that can be developed
Agreeing *ground rules* for working. Renegotiating or modifying rules.	Exploring conditions for good quality dialogue: listening, respect, taking turns, ensuring all included.
Sharing a *stimulus*: picture book, myth, legend or folk tale, poem, animation, photograph, painting, comic strip, newspaper article, TV programme.	Children invited to make a personal response. Working with the material focuses attention on the sequence of events in a story, on the detail of representation and the diversity of interpretations.
Thinking time – alone or in pairs and small groups with access to paper and pens/pencils.	Pupils consider own responses. Ideas developed on paper through drawings webs and brainstorms: writing a tool for thinking. Pupils express thinking in different ways.
Framing and sharing questions All children are involved in creating and choosing questions. Teacher pays attention to recording the questions in the pupils' own words, encouraging elaboration of the thinking behind each question.	Children offer their questions, recorded for all to see. Questions are clarified, connected and grouped by the participants, either working as a whole class or breaking into smaller groups. Pupils learn to refine questions and to recognise the most promising to discuss.

Involves text and media interrogation driven by readers'/listeners' responses

Building on ideas to develop dialogue in seeking to answer the questions chosen. Teacher's role is critical in offering questions to deepen the discussion and to promote progress, while holding back on her/his own view and avoiding taking the lead. Building is oral and recorded in the form of notes, lists and mind maps.	Pupils use a range of skills: making connections, comparisons and distinctions between ideas, offering examples and analogies, expressing opinions, agreeing and disagreeing with one another, giving reasons, constructing arguments and counter-arguments. Encourages listening and reasoning, develops critical and creative thinking and builds confidence. Allows participants to rehearse their ideas and to change their minds as a result of the dialogue.
Closure and review What progress has been made in answering the question? How well did we work together as a community of enquiry?	The class identifies provisional answers to their questions and often raise further questions. They reflect on their own participation, on the progress of the dialogue and their effectiveness as a community.

ACTION POINTS ACTION POINTS ACTION POINTS ACTION POINTS ACTION POINTS

The success of a philosophical approach to education depends on you doing the following:

> **offering rich and thought-provoking material to children to encourage questioning and talk;**

> **being willing to work at your skills of facilitation, particularly listening, questioning and responding tactfully to children's ideas;**

> **making flexible use of the framework and process of the community of enquiry as a means to support and strengthen collaborative dialogue.**

Conclusion

One of the strongest themes to emerge from children's comments on questioning and dialogue in the classroom is the value they place on having their ideas heard and taken seriously. One ten-year-old suggests that these discussions are different *'cos people don't laugh when you ask questions and people don't laugh because they all feel more relaxed and it's just easier to listen when you're relaxed*. They find the experience of philosophy stimulating and enjoyable, as well as useful in their everyday lives, as one girl reports: *I find the rules for philosophy useful when I go home because every time I go to shout at my brother I just use those rules to calm down* (Murris and Haynes, 2000, p83). An eleven-year-old boy from one London primary school told an audience of teachers at a conference: *At school, mostly teachers take over the lesson plans ... in philosophy children take over the lesson plan, and sometimes you don't even need a lesson plan ...* He described its position in his life: *You've got home and you've got school, and philosophy is sort of in between* (Haynes, 2006). Children acknowledge the impact the dialogue has on their thinking and value the opportunity to hear the views of others and engage in debate. One child suggested, *Everyone comes up with different ideas and it makes it better* and another boy in the same class enjoyed *having all the different arguments, finding out whether things are true or not and discussing them all together* (Murris and Haynes, 2000, p83).

This approach to teaching is now used by teachers in many countries. Its popularity has been growing for more than thirty years. Systematic studies have shown that sustained participation in open-ended enquiry leads to growth in learners' self-esteem and has a positive impact on cognitive and reasoning ability (SAPERE, 2006). Teachers report a wide variety of benefits when children take part regularly in this kind of thoughtful dialogue. These include improved listening, concentration, collaboration and increased confidence and ability to question and articulate ideas. Above all, if you adopt this philosophical approach in your teaching, you will enjoy time and space to reflect and listen to children's ideas and to join with them in compelling and often unexpected co-enquiries.

Further reading

Bradman, T. and Ross, T. (1990) *Michael*. London: Andersen Press.
A humorous and powerful portrayal of a boy who does not listen or do as he is told at school but still succeeds in his mission. The book is suitable for seven- to eleven-year-olds and essential reading for teachers.

Sendak, M. (1992) *Where the Wild Things Are*. London: Picture Lions.
This is a classic picture book by one of the best author illustrators of our time, a must for every Early Years and infant classroom. Max and the Wild Things evoke a strong response in readers of all ages.

Strauss, G. and Browne, A. (1993) *The Night Shimmy*. London: Random House.
A beautifully illustrated tale of a boy who creates the 'Night Shimmy' to speak on his behalf. This story touches on our struggles with fear and anger along with the importance of friendship.

Van Allsberg, C. (1984) *The Mysteries of Harris Burdick*. Boston, MA: Houghton Mifflin.
Suitable for older primary school children, this is a highly original book that immediately engages the reader in the mysteries portrayed through a series of haunting illustrations and captions.

Velthuijs, M. (1991) *Frog and the Birdsong*. London: Andersen Press.
Velthuijs' style of illustration never fails to draw children into the lives of his characters. The death of a blackbird sensitively opens the possibility for discussion with younger children.

References

Doddington, C. (2001) Entitled to speak: talk in the classroom, *Studies in Philosophy and Education*, 20, 267–74.
Fisher, R. (1990) *Teaching Children to Think*. Hemel Hempstead: Simon & Schuster Education.
Haynes, J. (2002) *Children as Philosophers: Learning Through Enquiry and Dialogue in the Primary Classroom*. London: Routledge.
Haynes, J. (2007) Freedom and the urge to think in philosophy with children, in *Gifted Education International, Special Edition on Philosophy with Children*, 22 (2/3), 229–38. Bicester: A.B. Academic Publishers.
Lipman, M. (1991) *Thinking in Education*. Cambridge: Cambridge University Press.
Lipman, M (ed.) (1993) *Thinking Children and Education*. Dubuque, IA: Kendall/Hunt.
Murris, K. and Haynes, J. (2000) *Storywise: Thinking Through Stories*. Newport: Dialogueworks.
SAPERE (Society for the Advancement of Philosophical Enquiry and Reflection in Education) (2006) *P4C Report for the Innovations Unit, January*. Oxford: Westminster Institute of Education, Oxford Brookes University.
Stanley, S. with Bowkett, S. (2004) *But Why? Developing Philosophical Thinking in the Classroom*. Stafford: Network Educational Press.

4
The joy of performance
John Burnett

Introduction

Producing, directing and performing a play with young children is not as difficult or challenging as it might initially appear. Young children generally love dressing up and acting out stories and will very readily take the lead from an enthusiastic class teacher willing to put aside some quality time over a few weeks for rehearsals. Your production can be a modest little affair practised for a week or two within the confines of the classroom and performed to other classes, parents and friends. It can, on the other hand, be a whole-school event, engaging teachers and parents in costume-making, designing lighting and composing music. Either way, a successful performance can prove a highlight in the life of a class or school community, as well as providing a medium for realising all sorts of curriculum-linked learning outcomes.

Fundamentally, doing a play means saying to the children, 'Let's tell our community a story through movement, mime, words and song'. Young children are not bedevilled with the self-consciousness which makes being on public view so painful for adolescents and some adults and this means they can act very easily. What they cannot do without adult support is sustain this natural ability and rehearse it in order to realise an effective performance. It is the teacher's ability to organise, see ahead and 'keep on trucking' when things get difficult which makes the whole thing happen and become a deeply satisfying experience for the whole school community.

Background

Classroom drama can take many forms. The case study outlined later in this chapter depicts a *choral play* where all the players are members of a chorus: speaking or singing together as a collective storyteller, while simultaneously observing the unfolding action of the story. Individuals take it in turn to step out of the group and become a character. When they have played their part, they melt back into the group and once more become storyteller and audience. The children remain continually engaged in the storytelling while individuals have scope for playing character parts without being overstretched. Using this formula, teachers can effectively introduce singing, movement, dance and recitation, together with parts for individuals who relish a challenge, provided this is done in such a way that the children do not get bored or marginalised (Price, 2005). The teacher using the medium of the choral play can be confident that rehearsals and the performance stay well disciplined for the children remain absorbed in the story they are telling. Being both audience and performers keeps everyone thoroughly engaged.

Choral drama has an ancient history. In the Athens of 400 BC, the drama was a religious festival involving the whole community seated in open-air amphitheatres (McCleish, 2003). Tragedies and comedies were ritualistic, using a Chorus which sang, danced and spoke in unison to the few individualised characters. Primary age children have a remarkable affinity with this dramatic form, which has its primal roots in much older shamanic dancing rituals of tribal people as well as in traditional circle games and the folk tradition of Mummer and Mystery Plays. In its simplest form, the choral drama is an inward activity, a ritualistic singing or recitation 'game' played for the satisfaction of the players alone without any audience. Less than half a century ago, children still played such games in the street and playground (Opie and Opie, 1985); many of the games like *The Farmer's in his Den* or the *Ally-Ally-Oo* were traditional street rituals passed down orally through generations. These traditions have been largely lost, swallowed up by a flood of television and digital entertainment but, in the hands of an enthusiastic teacher, it takes little to re-engage a group of children in new, choral drama. The process of re-engagement is particularly effective when the teacher is able to work with the class to produce simple play ideas, improvisations and home-grown scripts which can grow into exciting performances over a relatively short period of time (Pittis, 2003).

Organising a public performance

Public performance is part of our spectator culture. A football crowd chanting with their team, musicians firing up their audience at a concert, spectators urging on an Olympic athlete – in all these situations the same archetypal gesture appears: chorus in dialogue with individual players. Being in a crowd is a relatively safe experience; you can shout and roar and experience raw emotions without being exposed. Being the individual player is exhilarating and hugely rewarding but also challenging and potentially stressful. The choral play in the primary school provides a contained, collective space where children can actively participate in the emotional switchback of a good story presented through a range of media. At the same time, through the guidance and mentoring of an insightful teacher, individual children can be supported in stepping out of the circle, taking responsibility and expressing their own creativity in a safe and measured way.

Put aside the same time every day for rehearsal and repeat the play as a ritual. If the children have already memorised the words and songs, the play can unfold as a daily 'game' with established rules. Let your colleagues know when you will be rehearsing so you don't do an improvised battle scene when the neighbouring class have silent reading. Keep rehearsals short (30 minutes) and regular. You can have a play ready for performance in ten days if you practise every day.

TO THINK ABOUT

- Until the advent of television and digital entertainment, children's singing games were played quite spontaneously in primary school playgrounds.

- These traditional singing games told little stories through sung or recited choruses and children took turns to briefly play individual characters.

- The great dramas of Ancient Greece, medieval Mystery Plays and Mummer Plays all used the same form as the traditional singing game.

- Modern musicals like *Chitty Chitty Bang Bang* and *the Sound of Music* use the same formula for their productions.

ACTION POINT ACTION POINT ACTION POINT ACTION POINT ACTION POINT

Practise choral speaking in the classroom with the children repeating line by line from the teacher. Primary children can learn long speeches in a couple of days this way without needing a script. Everyone can learn the individual parts in the same way. This way they are all understudies and can take turns at playing individual parts.

Book the school hall if you are lucky enough to have access to one. If that is not possible, turn the classroom into a performance area and drill the children in quickly making a workable space by moving desks and classroom furniture. Have strict rules regarding movement during rehearsals. Make sure you know where each child will sit and stand and be clear about individual positioning when parts are played. Give the children precise indications at the first rehearsal and practise this until they are secure. When positions and movements are secure, they can then improvise without things falling into chaos. Map out the movements before you rehearse, not during the rehearsal. Think through the space in which the children will move and make it safe and predictable for them. You should consider the following points carefully.

- The *choral play*, using a speaking chorus or singing chorus, with individual characters stepping forth from a semi-circle and then rejoining the group after they have played their part is a particularly effective way of engaging primary children in performance art.
- Regular, rhythmic practice of a choral play gives the children security to improvise and be creative without stress.
- Choral plays are easy to write and can be tailored to suit the personalities of a particular class.
- Children need adults to help them realise an effective performance but can take ownership of the whole process if well rehearsed.
- Playing an individual role can be hugely formative for children and can have a positive influence on their adult development.
- Speaking and singing in chorus provides a secure medium through which a whole class can engage in the creative and ancient art of storytelling.

Look around for themes which will go well with the class and sketch out a series of scenes in which the whole class can take part. Involve the class in your ideas. If you start writing down some lines, they may well come up with scenes of their own. Write your own plays if possible and tailor them to the personalities in your class.

CASE STUDY 4.1

Class act

The class are quieter than I have ever known them. It is not a suppressed silence – they are bursting with excitement; their eyes are flashing and their faces flushed with concentration and excitement. They are literally trembling with anticipation. I lift the heavy curtain over the hall door and we hear the buzz of an audience waiting for the performance to begin.There is a capacity crowd. Mums and dads, grannies and siblings are all seated in the front rows eager for a good view of our play based on a tale from the Icelandic Edda but there are also visitors, ex-pupils, worthies from the town and friends of the school as this is an Open Day and we are on public show. We can hear the host teacher announcing our performance. She stops. The audience go still and suddenly we are on! I lift back the curtain, sound brief notes on my recorder and step back as the children pick up the melody, step in time and process into the hall.

As I watch the children singing and processing without any help from me, I know this is going to be a good performance. They have rehearsed this play to a point where they no longer need me as director or guide. My role as teacher is simply to see that the props and the benches are in place and that there are no obstacles on stage or in the narrow pathway leading to it. They move as one person; they are totally absorbed in the tale they are telling as they sing and speak in chorus. They have been practising the songs in procession every day for weeks, so there is no danger anyone will forget. Everybody knows everybody else's parts, so there are twenty-five prompters ready to jump in if someone falters. They have the total confidence of a well-drilled troupe of soldiers on parade. They know each other's faults and characters and the rehearsals have forged a powerful bond between them. They are an ensemble, working together for a performance, carrying each other's quirks, sharing each other's gifts and presenting this in the form of a ritualised, well rehearsed game. I can see from their eyes that they are loving every moment.

The children reach the semi-circle of benches placed carefully on the stage, each in his or her appointed place and they stand there, splendid, with the stage lights on their simple, coloured costumes. Each child has a crown, a simple strip of card, sprayed and joined with a paper clip, decorated with spirals and patterns of string emulating Nordic designs. Some, playing the part of the gods, have winged side pieces; the giants – the 'baddies' of the story – have square, heavy shapes; the goddesses have fine bracelets and jewellery, lovingly wrought out of paper and sweet-wrappers in one of our afternoon lessons.

The play unfolds like clockwork. I watch from the side, following every move but not interfering. For thirty minutes they hold the stage, using the ancient theatrical form of the choral play – a chorus with individual characters stepping forth from a semi-circle and then rejoining the group after they have played their part. The audience laugh; then they become hushed and are clearly engaged. Adults can often be patronising when watching children on stage, but on this occasion they are carried along by the magic of children, totally absorbed in the dramatic ritual. The play speeds up to a climax; the chorus chants with rising pace, telling how Iduna and her rescuer, Loki, the mischief-maker, flee from the ice-giants on magic wings. Slipping into fluttering, crepe-paper wings, with outspread arms, they leap off the stage and tear through the audience who gasp with surprise. Thundering after them comes Thiassi, the ice-giant. The three characters disappear out of the back of the hall and the entire chorus rush forward, following the players with their eyes. The audience's heads swivel as the escapers rush in through another door and race back to the stage. Like commentators in an Olympic race the chorus builds up the tension:

Swifter, swifter

Swoops the eagle

Now their strength begins to fail

Can they reach

The fiery beacon?

Can they gain

Valhalla's heights?

It is mere doggerel but the children live in the scene with all their energy. The heroine and her rescuer stagger onto stage and the ice-giant falls, swallowed in flames.

The tale has been told; the universe is put back in order and the children, still wrapped in the ritual of the story-game, led by Odin, king of the gods, take up the melody of their processional song and march out of the hall in time and in tune. The well-practised routine of song, movement and choral speech has held them safely. Within this form, all the little improvisations made by individual characters have had a chance to shine but, essentially, the past thirty minutes have been a group event, the united voice and face of a class of ten-year-olds performing and presenting collective art.

I shepherd them quickly to their classroom and then they explode! No longer players in ancient dramatic ritual, they are now bouncing, modern ten-year-olds, exhilarated with the satisfaction that they have put on a great performance. We have to work hard to protect their costumes as they fling them off in the hurry to see their parents. They know they have done well and the comments from parents and colleagues tell us that all the work in rehearsal has been worth it. Packing up the last costume and putting the last crown away in a box for some future performance, I feel some sadness that the play has come to an end but also quiet satisfaction that we, the class, the teacher and the whole school community, achieved something memorable; something which not only entertained the audience but linked the children to the very roots of their human culture.

In the humblest class play, children can reveal aspects of themselves which no one knew existed. A successful play can aid the self-development of individuals and do wonders for the self-esteem of a whole group.

The long-term impact of performance

Although the performance of 'Iduna's Apples' took place nearly thirty years ago I like to think that the players, now approaching their forties, still remember the performance as vividly as I do. It was one of many plays that I and the class performed together over a number of years but on that particular occasion, both teacher and class knew something special was happening. It was a point where the creativity of class and teacher gelled. We sang, recited, moved and told a story together and were all members of the same team. We enjoyed every minute of the rehearsals and the performance was one big, super-charged festival. The following week it was back to the regularity of Maths and English practice, but it did not matter. We had been to a magic land and had taken all our friends and relatives with us for a short visit. The boat we had sailed in was made out of the collective goodwill generated by our wish to put on a performance and show what we as a learning community were made of. It was also built out of tolerance, imagination and enthusiasm. We could work harder and better because of all we had shared together.

As they grew up, the class community of which I was teacher kept in touch. When they reached the age of thirty they arranged a reunion and invited me, their class teacher, and their high-school mentor to the party. It was a powerful experience, seeing these professional men and women who now had families and were making their way in the world. The spirit of the class group, that tangible entity which had worked with me on the play so many years ago, was still there, now woven into their maturing personalities and spread across the many different countries in which they now worked and lived.

The same joking mood I knew when they were young, the same status games, the same sparky dialogues were rattling around the group. My colleague and I, now well into our fifties, were called home from the party by our wives at one o'clock in the morning. As we walked down the road to the car, the whole class came out on the pavement to wish us goodbye. I will never forget the look in their eyes. It was not sentimental or reverential, but the gaze exchanged between friends who have shared important things together and remained there for each other.

Last year, at a conference in London, I met the girl who took the part of Iduna in the play. As a small child she was reserved and shy but in rehearsals she found the courage to hold a big part, be the heroine and hurl herself into space, flapping a huge pair of paper wings. She is now a mother of two, a professional viola player and active with a pioneer school in Greenwich. The boy who played Loki became a 'squaddie' in the SAS. At school he was clever, inventive and always ready to take risks. He was a definite leader with a flair for mischief. He was active in the Gulf War but his work is classified. A few weeks ago, I received a card from the girl who played Odin, the king of the gods. She tells me she is now teaching and taking a post as a class teacher. Of all the children in the play, she was the one who kept us all together. I could not have produced it without her support. I hope she will perform plays with her class.

ACTION POINT ACTION POINT ACTION POINT ACTION POINT ACTION POINT

> Decide on a number of scenes which tell a clear story. Use a chorus to speak or sing the narrative with individuals stepping out from the choral group. The play should be no longer than thirty minutes to make it manageable.

How working with choral plays will impact on your teaching

Working with choral plays will provide you with huge satisfaction in your teaching, offering a medium that you will find easy to work with and that is healthy for young children. As well as having a lot of fun with the class, you will find it easy to realise a host of 'desirable outcomes' with a minimum of strain. You cannot produce a play without concentrated speaking and listening; children directly engage in writing and reading scripts. The challenge of speaking lines from memory or improvising when things go wrong (as they always do) is something hesitant readers often excel in. You will find that the parts the children play and the discipline they acquire in realising a performance will give them confidence to both stand alone and work as a team. This confidence is something they can take with them into adolescence, into their private and professional lives as adults. Performance art is a powerful medium for achieving this. Writing and producing a play is a hugely satisfying thing for a teacher, especially if the children join in the process. Both teacher and class gain confidence in their creative abilities, not only as actors but also as singers, musicians, designers, painters of scenery and makers of props. There is something in it for everyone.

The performance, even a modest event in the classroom performed for the class next door, is a celebration of what a team can achieve through sharing their gifts and working on developing new skills. As you and the class gain confidence in each other's creative abilities you can combine forces with other teachers and produce a play in which the whole school community is involved. When this is going well your work helps build the ethos of your school, in the same way as does the coaching of the football team, rehearsing a little choir or tending the school garden.

TO THINK ABOUT
TO THINK ABOUT

When things go wrong in a performance, it can be the best bit of learning. If you encourage the children to improvise when someone forgets their lines or the scenery falls down, you will be amazed at the level of creativity and enjoyment experienced by the cast. Learning not to panic when the system fails is an excellent training for life.

Conclusion

A child is a bit like Aladdin's lamp – you only need to polish it a little bit and all sorts of magical forces come rushing out, often in the most unlikely and deprived circumstances. Among other qualities, these forces confer the gift of imagination, that essentially human capacity which can look with empathy towards the future and find new, creative ways of being active in the world.

Children growing up to cope with an uncertain future will need to find these magical forces in themselves. They will be best helped in this through having teachers who share their enthusiasms for the good, creative things in life. Doing plays is one sure way of awakening their power of imagination. It is also a medium where children can grow as social beings, learning to give and take in the service of something greater and more important than their personal selves. With the play, this medium is the performance; in the broader field of things, it is life itself.

> **Key Quote**
> *Participation in creative drama has the potential to develop language and communication abilities, problem-solving skills, and creativity; to promote a positive self-concept, social awareness, empathy, a clarification of values and attitudes, and an understanding of the art of theatre. Creative drama requires both logical and intuitive thinking, personalizes knowledge, and yields aesthetic pleasure.* (Davis and Evans, 1987)

References and further reading

Davis, J.H. and Evans, M.J. (1987) *Theatre, Children and Youth*. New Orleans, LA: Anchorage Press. Recognised as the standard textbook in the field of theatre for young audiences and a very useful book for teachers. (See website 'The Drama/Theatre Continuum'.)

Johnstone, K. (1999). *Impro for Storytellers*. New York: Routledge/Theatre Arts Books. As a long-time master of the art of improvisation, Keith Johnstone's writings are highly recommended for anyone interested in spontaneous drama, especially the unscripted humour which so often accompanies it.

McLeish, K. (2003) *Guide to Greek Theatre and Drama*. London: A. & C. Black. An authoritative and energetic introduction to the theatre of Ancient Greece.

Opie, I. and Opie, P. (1985) *Children's Games in Street and Playground*. Oxford: Oxford University Press. A wonderful classic, recording children playing and inventing chasing, catching, exerting, racing, duelling, daring, guessing, acting and pretending games.

Pittis, M.A. (2003) *Pedagogical Theatre: Dramaturgy and Performance Practice for Lower and Middle School Grades*. New York: AWSNA. Arthur Pittis teaches in a Rudolf Steiner school and writes with sustained enthusiasm about creating and adapting plays for classes.

Price, C. (2005) *Let's Do a Play: Eleven Class Plays for Grades 1–5 with Musical Accompaniments*. New York: AWSNA Colin Price, also a Steiner educator, shows how the teacher with a musical inclination can combine composing with play-writing.

5
Joyful history
Bill Leedham and Mike Murphy

Introduction

Did history bore you at school? Was it just a long list of names and dates? Or were you a fan of the 'horrible histories', revelling in the dirty deeds of the past? It is very tempting to play the scary card when faced with a restless class on a Friday afternoon but it's a law of diminishing returns. Attila the Hun may have been pretty frightening in his day but there's nothing in remoter times to compare with the industrialised killing of the Holocaust, and those hairy Vikings who spent all their time raping, pillaging and plundering are just creatures of the movie-maker's imagination. Read on if you want to use history to help children become fair-minded and independent citizens. If you just prefer the 'nasty bits', skip to another chapter!

TO THINK ABOUT

TO THINK ABOUT

Here is a selection of quotations from primary age children when they were asked what they thought about History.

It's what we are and what we want to be.

It's about us all and what we did and where we live.

It's about things that have happened that we don't want to forget and about the facts that happened in the olden days.

It's about my gran's life and her memories and her experiences.

It's about my life and what I feel and see and do.

History is like a big sack, filled up with stories and opinions about the past.

Key Quote
History is not events, but people. And it is not just people remembering, it is people acting and living their past in the present. (Jacob Bronowski, 1974, p438)

Lies, damn lies and history

Everyone knows that Henry VIII had six wives. Or did he? Wife number one was his brother's widow and Henry was correct when he asserted that divine law made the marriage incestuous. Henry's second marriage was also annulled as he had previously had an affair with the lady's sister. Marriage number three might have been valid as wives one and two were dead but in the eyes of Catholic Europe Henry was an excommunicant – incapable of taking part in any religious service. The same objection could be made to Henry's last three marriages and there were additional impediments in the case of wives four and five. While wife number four had already been promised to someone else (and the king found her repugnant in bed), wife number five had had lovers before she married the King and so was already married in the eyes of the Church. So how many wives did Henry have?

Children love this kind of 'debunking' of accepted truth because they feel that they have been let into a secret, something that most people don't know. They are fascinated to discover that there is a deeper level of fact beyond the superficial 'soundbite' history that is so popular on television. But be warned: once aware of it they are unlikely to be satisfied with anything less.

'That's all very well,' you may be saying, 'but do I have to be an expert on the Tudors to teach at Key Stage 2?' The answer is of course 'no', but history needs to make some sense to you if you are to make sense of it for others. If you find yourself having to teach an unfamiliar historical period, just imagine that you are taking the children on a holiday to that era back in time. You will tell the youngest ones where they will be staying and what the food is like, what the people wear and where they live; you will point out any obvious differences (e.g. no electric light or running water perhaps) and warn of any particular dangers (people throwing refuse out of the window). You will tell the older ones more about the way of life of the people and you might begin to tell them something about the history of the place, explaining why they do things differently from us. At every stage you will encourage the children to see the people of the past as real, entitled to be treated with respect and not caricatured in comic strip form. We may not get to know them as well as our contemporaries but through art, drama and music we can share creative experiences with them. Our first case study shows how this can be done.

CASE STUDY 5.1

Looking at a king

Show your class one of Holbein's magnificent portraits of Henry VIII on the whiteboard. Most junior age children will respond at once even if they can't name the king: *he's rich*; *he's big*; *he's old*; *he's fierce*; *he's tough* are just some of the comments you will hear. Some children will be more specific: *he's a king*; *he's on a throne*; *he has special clothes*; *he's wearing jewels*. You can use these first impressions to get the children to think more deeply. You might ask questions.

- *Is he angry?*

- *Is he a giant?*

- *Did he eat a lot?*

- *Did he live a long time ago?*

- *Was he married?*

- *Did he have children?*

- *Did he live in a palace?*

- *Did he have servants?*

This one pictorial source will therefore provide material for further exploration, discovery and learning.

Now tell the children that they are about to interview Henry VIII as reporters or journalists. They can work in pairs or larger groups and try their questions out on each other, each child taking on the role of the King. You will find that they have ideas about the 'right' answers to their own questions which can generate quite a lively debate. But who is right? Be ready to play the part of referee, a role which you might find quite rewarding, especially if you have the right resources to back up your arbitration!

Next, invite the children to compare Henry VIII's position with that of some modern celebrities. What roles do the celebrities play in society and how do these roles compare with his? Henry had to be prime minister, general, archbishop and captain of the England rugby team, simultaneously! Small wonder that the image he projected was larger than life. Once the children have begun to understand what a Tudor king needed to be successful they can build up a class display where Henry is surrounded by images of contemporary 'stars' and personalities whose achievements match his. Such an approach provides a host of opportunities for talk and expressive language and gives a good chance of success for all children at the start of a topic.

Thrills without spills

Among academic historians the word *imagination* has a doubtful reputation. When it comes to joyful history, however, it is your greatest asset and ally. Without it a visit to 'Tudor-land' (for example) would be impossible. Moreover, it is important to remember why we possess this remarkable facility and why its exercise is good for young minds. Educationalists emphasise the value of 'real experience' but in times gone by real experience might be very costly (for instance, your first encounter with a mammoth could be your last!). Imagination enables us to picture situations in our heads and to work out our reactions to them before we actually have to deal with them. It is no accident that imagination is at its strongest in childhood when the outside world is at its most dangerous and the need to learn is most intense. Nor can it be a coincidence that so many children find using their imagination enjoyable. A surprising amount of what is helpful to us in life is precisely that, enjoyable!

What we are not doing here is giving free reign to fantasy. History requires a disciplined use of the imagination, one that subjects its products to the test of evidence. We shouldn't think of the Vikings as horned and hairy because there is no evidence that they were and we should treat the evidence we do have about them as biased because most of it comes from their enemies, to whom they were the terrorists of the Dark Ages.

But we should also remember that the way we see history is changing. This does not just mean that it is now being written from many different points of view, for example 'black' history or women's history. It also means that evidence is becoming available in forms and quantities unknown to previous generations of historians. This gives the subject a dynamic feel, which is very different from the crusty image it used to have.

Take the case of the famous pharaoh, Tutankhamun. A painted box found in his tomb shows him furiously engaged in battle, but the archaeologists who first examined his mummy thought him rather too frail to be the warrior that the paintings suggest. X-rays taken of his corpse in the 1980s appeared to show skull fragments inside his brain cavity, suggesting that the young king was hit over the head. More recently we discovered that he suffered a broken leg shortly before his death, the final cause of which was septicaemia. Perhaps he was an 'action-man' after all!

Modern accounts of Tutankhamun's life reveal a change of perspective too. Nowadays scholars tend to emphasise that Egypt was a Bronze Age culture in which magic played a hugely important role. Country and monarch were one and the same: if the rituals of king-ship were not properly carried out the precarious balance between the forces of order and chaos would be upset and disaster would surely follow. You might think that such ideas are too difficult but part of the process of growing up means confronting the differ-ence between people and cultures and the reasons for them: there is no value in being taken on trips into the past if the only people we meet are ourselves in fancy dress.

Beginning at the beginning: Key Stage 1

So much for the 'facts', what about methods? There is no doubt that humans learn best by doing: it is what our brains are for. The authors find sitting still and listening very hard and we have had a lifetime to practise it! For young children without our level of self-control it is harder still. How then do we make history into a 'doing' subject?

Earlier we suggested that children's learning of history might be seen as a kind of 'coach tour' of the territories of the past. We also argued that the length of time to be spent in each 'land' would determine the knowledge needed to survive and the kind of activities needed to acquire this knowledge. The youngest children can work at a very visual and tangible level: a drawing, preferably labelled, tells us how well a young child has identi-fied the defining qualities of the thing observed. Thus Henry VIII is stout, with a gold chain round his neck, wide puffed-out sleeves and an assertive, masculine stance; William the Conqueror has his cross-hatched coat of mail.

Looking through the family photograph album will help to refine a child's power of observation, as will visits to historic houses or walks around the neighbourhood. Old objects brought into the classroom will assist in establishing the idea of change. You won't need to tell the children that things were done differently in the past because they come to school already knowing that Cinderella didn't have a mobile phone!

Our second case study shows how you can use children's love of a good story to start them on the process of becoming historians.

CASE STUDY 5.2

Who was that?

In through the classroom door bursts a figure all dressed in red. It is clearly Santa Claus. Behind him are two elves – Santa's helpers. The faces on some of the children look as if they are about to burst. Santa sits down and starts telling them about his Christmas: where he went, who he met, some of the weirdest and funniest presents he had to deliver. It is a story of adventure, recited at speed, but to help bring the story to life he dis-plays objects picked up on his travels, gifts given to him by some of the people and children he has met. He has also had photographs and notes left to him by children who were sleeping on Christmas Eve or by their parents before they went to bed. He shows the children pictures of some of the presents he liked best. He even has a little bag of leftovers which contain some of the snacks that have been left out for him. Some of Santa's stories are happy ones, while others are a bit sad.

Then a third elf bursts in from the corridor, shouting that the reindeer are threatening to revolt because the Christmas holidays are over and they want to go back to Lapland immediately. The elves say that if they do not go now, Santa Claus will be stranded in the school and if that happens there will be no Christmas presents ready for next year. With only a quick wave and shout of 'Ho ho ho', Santa and his helpers are gone.

Have the children imagined Santa's visit? Did it really happen? Still in a state of great surprise and some excitement they look around. In his haste to get away Santa has dropped some bags, which contain notes and pictures. He has also left behind strong memories and impressions.

As the class teacher you start to look around the room. The children are less stunned now and starting to buzz with talk. You look at them searchingly and ask: 'What was that all about?' However, before you allow children to start answering they are asked to close their eyes for a minute or so while they try to remember the events of the morning. You tell them it is essential that they think really hard to remember what was said and what happened, because some very serious detective work now needs to be done.

This dramatic event was set up by two teachers who were teaching mixed age classes across Years 2, 3 and 4. They used the Santa scenario to stimulate historical thinking on a number of levels and to promote and encourage historical knowledge, skills and understanding. Over time all of the following areas were included: understanding chronology; corroboration and memory; exploratory talk, oral history and writing; facts and opinions; myths and stories – evidence and interpretation; artefacts; reliability, bias and alternative points of view; first- and second-hand sources; questions about what is history; ways of recording history and historical events.

A similar example would be to use 'The mystery of the bag' approach. A bag has been found which contains various items, such as a wallet, passport, theatre tickets and so on. Some deductions – for example the gender of the owner of the bag – can be positively determined; others may be merely guesswork. Using evidence in this way allows the children to see how tentative historical judgements have to be. When the truth is revealed they will quickly realise the need for critical thinking.

Making progress: Key Stage 2

Asking questions is the professional historian's main role in life and questioning lies at the heart of school history too, though there are different kinds of response. Questions that end in a description or a drawing can be described as 'What?' questions, while those that encompass a process or procedure generally start 'How?' Questions which begin with 'Why?' are of a different order as they demand explanation, which as we noted earlier requires an understanding of context. As we saw in the example of Tutankhamun, 'Why' questions also take us into the realm of speculation and of possible alternatives, where knowledge of the culture may be as important as knowledge of the facts.

At this point it is necessary for you to be aware of a divergence of opinion among academic historians. There are some who think that we can never enter into the psychology of people in the past, while others think it essential if we are to understand why they did what they did. Here, for example, is the Pharaoh Rameses II (1279–1213 BC) in a tight spot.

> *Then his majesty arose like the war god his father and put on his armour. He charged forward and plunged into the midst of his enemies, the detested Hittites. He was alone and there was no one beside him as he charged. When he looked around he saw there were 2,500 chariots surrounding him – all the bravest soldiers in the Hittite army. No captain stood with his majesty, no soldier of the army, no shield-bearer. Then said his majesty 'What is wrong with you, my father Amun? Is it a father's part to ignore a son? Have I done anything without you? Do I not walk or halt as you tell me? Have I not made for you many monuments and filled your temple with spoils? What will men say if harm befalls one who follows your advice always?'* (From an inscription on the temple wall at Abu Simbel)

Setting aside the strange names and rather elaborate language, what is King Rameses saying? Basically he is telling the god Amun that a god who lets down his worshippers has no future. This is the *quid pro quo* that underlay all ancient religion and is still part of everyday speech. 'Don't count your chickens', we say or 'touch wood', in an attempt to get Fate on our side. Rameses built temples; some of us still give up chocolate for Lent.

From a very different time and place comes a letter from a young man called William Paston, a 17-year-old schoolboy at Eton in 1478 writing to his elder brother John, the head of the family in London.

> *Right reverend and worshipful brother, I recommend me unto you, desiring to hear of your welfare and prosperity ... My tutor, Master Thomas, heartily recommends himself to you and prayeth you to send him some money for my commons; for he saith ye be 20 shillings in his debt for a month was already due when he had money last. Also I beseech you to send me a hose cloth, one for the holidays of some colour and another for working days, how coarse it be maketh no matter ... And if it like you that I may come by water and sport me with you at London a day or two this term time, then ye may let all this be tell the time that I come.*
>
> *Written the Saturday after All Hallowe'en Day with the hand of your brother, William Paston.*

At first sight this letter seems very difficult yet it too is easy to understand once the barrier of language is overcome. What William wants is some new clothes and a chance to spend some 'quality time' with John. A modern rendering of the text might go as follows:

> *Hi bro, hope all is OK with you. Just to remind you you owe my tutor twenty quid for my board and lodgings, plus the twenty you owe him for last month. While you're at it, could you send me some new jeans – a pair for school and a pair for going out in? If I can get up to London we can go clubbing and you can give me them then. Your mate, Will.*

The point about this and the Rameses passage is that they act as bridges, ways in which we can establish common ground with the people in the past, just as we would try to do if we were meeting with a stranger. Why otherwise would English people famously open a conversation by talking about the weather? Once we know the stranger is friendly we can begin to enquire about their world, find out what it is like to live in 'Paston-land'. Of course there will be difficulties: Will was also a child of his time. Here he writes to his brother about a girl he has met:

> *As for the young gentlewoman, I will tell you how I first got to know her. Her father is dead but she has two sisters. I was at the elder sister's wedding with my landlady who told them all about me. Her home is in London but she came to a house of theirs near Eton to be close to the wedding. Next Monday she will go to the Pardon at Sheen. As for the money and plate it is ready whenever she is wedded but the estate may not be hers until her mother dies. Regarding her beauty you can judge when you see her. Look at her hands especially, as some people say she is disposed to be fat.*

Being a younger son with no prospects Will was on the lookout for a wealthy wife – no real mystery here – but the mention of a 'Pardon' takes us into the controversy which brought about the Reformation: the practice of selling indulgences to those seeking a short cut to Heaven. One of the most famous characters in literature, Chaucer's Pardoner, was in this lucrative trade. Perhaps Will's prospective bride was interested in some cut-price offers.

Are we venturing way beyond Key Stage 3 at this point, let alone Key Stage 2? To understand Will Paston's world you just need to get inside his head. What do we know that he did not? Without the scientific discoveries of the last 500 years our ideas would be much the same as his. Indeed, one of the more joyful aspects of joyful history is to discover that people in the past were not nearly as mad, bad or sad as they appear to be, just operating on the basis of different information. And you can be sure that our ideas will look pretty daft in the year AD 2500!

Our final case study shows how this approach helped a Cornish school celebrate its own connection with the scientific revolution that brought the modern world into being.

CASE STUDY 5.3

Real lives, real people

The engine house looks like it's dead, and all its life has gone. The window holes look like eye spaces. I liked learning about the time when the engine house was alive and real. I've looked at it and drawn it and written a poem about how it was left to die in the field down by the River Tamar. The miners worked so hard in them under the ground, but look at it now! We humans just like changing stuff; I suppose it's called the future. (Kate, a pupil in Year 6)

There had been a real buzz throughout a small primary school in Cornwall during the second half of the summer term, and now the day had arrived and the children were going to tell their whole village about the life and times of the eighteenth and nineteenth-century inventor and engineer, Richard Trevithick (1771–1833). Weeks of research and creativity were about to be celebrated with the whole community.

The school had used the life and achievements of Richard Trevithick as a starting point for work across the whole curriculum, which involved local history, language and traditions as well as the industry of the area, its geography and economy, all of which were explored through music, art, poetry and folklore, along with visits to museums, galleries and other forms of outdoor learning. Science and technology brought in a local 'young engineers group', organised by some knowledgeable and enthusiastic parents. As part of the theme it was a natural development to place local knowledge and learning within the wider national historical perspective. Through a variety of cross curricular approaches the children were able to become immersed in deeper ideas of the time, which went beyond dates and key events. They grew in confidence (as did the teachers through their collaborative work) and by the end of the project all had a sense of their own expertise as historians. This was a poem Matt (Year 5) wrote in the 'Cinquain' style:

Trevithick, giant engineer

Dreamer, inventor

Adventurer

Puffing steam machines pumping

Cornish.

Key issues which were explored included: the main changes that took place during the Industrial Revolution and how people were affected by them; differences between town and country; differences between rich and poor; whether it was a good time to live or not. In addition, further questions regarding notions of citizenship, nationalism, ethnicity, regionalism and identity were considered in appropriate ways. So after a group of children explained to the other pupils gathered on the school field how they had researched and constructed their own beam engine based on Trevithick's principles, the afternoon was concluded with the children from Year 4 singing a rousing version of *The Song of the Western Men*, also known as *Trelawny*, published in 1824 and written by Robert Stephen Hawker (1803–75). The song is always heard at Cornish rugby matches and other Cornish gatherings and it is known as the unofficial Cornish anthem.

Conclusion

At the end of the project about Trevithick, a teacher, commented:

One of the best things about teaching a theme in this way was that we [the teachers] had a real opportunity to plan, explore ideas and teach and support each other as a team, while the children could also learn from each other. In this sense the approach produced a real sense of collaboration. We just felt like a real learning community, not a school, but a special place to be, and the whole experience allowed all the children to really contribute and participate; but what I enjoyed most was watching children thrive and have fun, everyone had fun, but it was real learning.

Where does all this leave us in terms of the National Curriculum? We have seen that truth matters but it can be approached in layers. We have seen that without the ability to link the experiences of the people of the past with their own children see history as no more than a series of names and dates, but we have also become aware that with the right resources the past becomes a country less different from our own than we might think. Will Paston can be seen walking into the gates of the Community College near where the authors work. He would still like to make his fortune without really trying and still like the kind of girl the other guys admire. Moreover, whether he thinks about it very much or not, he would still like to think he was a 'decent bloke' who knows right from wrong, even if he has a much vaguer idea of how God fits into the picture. If asked the biggest question of all: 'Who are you?' he is still likely to answer much as the original Will would have done, in terms of school, family, district or country. In other words joyful history is not just about truth, it is also about the making of friends. Our case studies show three ways in which this can be done, while equipping children to think critically and ask searching questions. It is a habit, once acquired, that will last a lifetime.

Further reading

Cooper, H. (2004) *The Teaching of History in Primary Schools*. London: David Fulton.
The latest edition of the most popular guide to primary history teaching published in the last 15 years, fully updated to take account of changes to the National Curriculum and the reports of HM Inspectors.

Davies, J. and Redmond, J. (1998) *Co-ordinating History Across the Primary School*. Abingdon: Falmer Press.
A lively and comprehensive guide for those who seek to lead the teaching of history forward in primary schools.

Husbands, C. (1996) *What Is History Teaching?* Buckingham: Open University Press.
A challenging introduction to an ongoing debate which combines theory and practice across the key stages.

Turner-Bisset, R. (1996) *History in the Primary Classroom*. London: David Fulton.
Many ideas are developed in this book, which reminds us that history is essentially a creative subject.

References

The full text of the Kadesh inscription of Rameses II can be found at:
http://www.touregypt.net/battleofkadesh
The text of Will Paston's letter to his brother can be found in R. Virgoe (1989) *Illustrated Letters of the Paston Family*. London: Macmillan, p263.

6
The joy of teaching and learning geography
Margaret Mackintosh

Introduction

You have almost certainly noticed that geography gets a bad press, especially when compared with history. Geographical programmes on television usually carry a travel, tourism or adventure label, Michael Palin's *Himalaya* and *Sahara* for example, whereas history programmes are advertised explicitly as 'history' or 'archaeology'. The only time the word 'geography' seems to be mentioned is to preface questions in quiz programmes, such as *Weakest Link*. For instance: '... and in geography what is the most southwesterly county in England?' This tendency reinforces the mistaken impression that geography is only about the location of places and names of capital cities, longest rivers and highest mountains. But, although geographical general knowledge like this is important, geography is much more than this. It is also much more exciting and interesting. Geography is about environments and the people who live and work in them or who visit them for different reasons. It is about how people the world over interact with and change their environment, how the environment influences their way of life and their culture. It is about how people live today, but also about how people's actions today will or could affect the lives and environments of future generations. (This aspect of geography is often called 'futures'.)

Geography is, literally, all around every one of us – it is an integral part of our everyday lives. Children experience it at all times as they play and move around in their world. Children also enjoy learning about real people. This chapter shows how the everyday or personal geographies of children in your class and of people around the world can be brought into your classroom in creative ways to enthuse both you and your pupils. Fieldwork is essential and drama invaluable in teaching and learning geography, but these are discussed in Chapters 4 and 7 on 'performance' and 'outdoor education', so I'm going to focus here on two aspects that I think open up the subject to all learners in a creative and enthusing way, namely on the *use of visual images* (being graphicate) and on *talk* (being orate).

Background

When one of the two primary project leaders of the national Action Plan for Geography was interviewed she was asked, *What does geography mean to you?* She replied: *The way I connect to the world, my global relationships, the way I navigate my world, the way my actions affect the planet* (North, 2006, p21). The other was asked, *How important do you think geography is today?* She replied:

> *Geography is of immeasurable importance. It just gets into everything. Everything we do, we do in a context that involves a complex web of people and places with all sorts of implications. All our lives are just one big geographical puzzle and I believe that when we try to relate ourselves to the bigger picture we can make sense of our place in the world more easily. Geography offers us the skills to understand and tackle many of today's big issues such as poverty, inequality, pollution, multi-cultural understanding and energy needs.* (Owens, 2006, p12)

One of the most important things for children to study is the world in which they live, to help them begin to make sense of their world, from their everyday, local world to the global world of the big picture. Geography includes aspects of the *scientific*: collecting and handling data and testing hypotheses in geographical enquiries, but it also includes the *humanistic*: personal views, beliefs, opinions and reactions to places and events. Increasingly it includes the *radical*: critical questioning of the key concepts of the global dimension – global citizenship, conflict resolution, diversity, human rights, interdependence, social justice, sustainable development and values and perceptions (DFID, 2005). These topics manifest themselves in issues such as fair trade, 'Making Poverty Permanent' (*sic*), migration and accessibility of clean water (Palfrey, 2006). This introduces one of the strengths and joys of geography: that there are very often, unlike in the rest of the curriculum, no 'right' answers. There are ideas and opinions to be presented, justified, explored, challenged, argued about and voted upon. This tentativeness brings excitement and interest into the classroom. You, the teacher, might initially feel insecure in this 'not knowing the answer' context, as might some children, but others thrive on it and it does lead to powerful geography.

Joyless geography

No, I am not going to describe a case study of what I consider to be poor practice. You have probably seen and recognised it. It can be summarised as 'death by worksheet' or perhaps 'death by PowerPoint'. I'm sure you know what I mean. Perhaps Key Stage 1 children, following a short walk or field trip, have been given a photograph and a line drawing of their local shops. They cut out the labels, stick them on, hopefully in appropriate places, and then colour in the picture. Five minutes cutting, sticking and thinking geographically, 25 minutes colouring! Similarly, whatever the experiences the Key Stage 2 children have had – perhaps a field trip or a television programme, interesting or not – too often they have to write it all down or fill in blanks on a worksheet that some of them struggle to read. The geography lesson becomes a literacy lesson, so those struggling with literacy are doomed to fail at geography too. Pupils very quickly learn that the more they notice or become interested in, the more they will have to write, the more curious they become, the more questions they will have to formulate and eventually answer. Their interest and curiosity is quickly stifled and they are turned off geography. As teacher, you find it so disappointing that, even if you were initially enthusiastic, this becomes short-lived. Joyless learning and joyless teaching become a downward spiral.

ACTION POINT ACTION POINT ACTION POINT ACTION POINT ACTION POINT

> Death *to* unnecessary worksheets in geography, not death *by* worksheet, please!

I have mentioned colouring. In a 1991 BBC video on *Teaching Geography*, David Bellamy asked some primary children, 'What is geography?' After responses such as, 'Science, hard science' and 'Learning about the rest of the world', one girl tilted her head to one side and said, 'It's art, sort of modern art', and you knew just what her geography lessons were like: colouring in incomprehensible maps or meaningless flags.

TO THINK ABOUT

What do *you* think the children are learning? What do *they* think they are learning? Perhaps they are making a poster about a locality or environmental issue; if so, are they thinking and learning geography or art? Perhaps they are completing a worksheet or writing an account, albeit in a geographical context; if so, are they thinking and learning geography or literacy? Perhaps they are making a model of a landscape feature; if so, are they thinking and learning geography or design and technology? Ask yourself whether or not the children are thinking geographically or in some other curriculum area. Remember that their perceptions may be different from your own.

CASE STUDY 6.1

Gambia

Children in a Year 1 class were moving freely around their classroom, enthusiastically handling a collection of everyday, mostly domestic, artefacts from the Gambia. The teacher was observing their activity, eavesdropping on their excited conversations, noting the vocabulary they used, the questions they asked each other and their speculation about each object: what? who? where? how? why? when? The children worked out, with some teacher help, what each artefact was used for, who might use it, where it might be obtained from and where it might be used. They identified what it was made from and suggested why these particular materials were used. They thought about when it might be used. They matched and compared each artefact with the equivalent artefacts from their western life. After the children had worked out how each Gambian item might be used, the teacher sequenced the items so that, as the children acted out each in use to a tape of Gambian music, they created a story. The story was of a Gambian meal, from the starting point of growing vegetables in the women's gardens (we would call them allotments), to shopping in the market, collecting water from a well and fuel wood from the bush, preparing the meal, cooking it in an aluminium pot on a wood fire and eating it. They had great fun, gained some idea of a Gambian way of life and used their own everyday geographical experiences of a market or a garden to help them understand more distant geography.

To conclude their simulation of a Gambian day, they ate a suitably adjusted Gambian meal (mostly tomatoes, onion and rice – and definitely no peanuts, peanut oil or chilli peppers) in communal Gambian style, eight pupils around each bowl of food. Instead of their right hand – very messy as, without practice, the food squeezes between your fingers – they used teaspoons. The afternoon finished with 'Grace and Family', a story about the Gambia, which helped the children to contextualise what they had been doing.

Sometime later the use of the artefacts was revisited with the school council members, three representatives from each year. In addition, these children watched a video clip about a Gambian market and another about one particular village compound. From photographs they explored what each member of the extended Muslim family would do from dawn to dusk. They developed a simulation of 'A day in the life of Lamin Darboe's compound' (Lamin is a Gambian who lives with his extended family in a village near the capital city, Banjul) and acted it out to the whole school. The purpose of this activity was for them to recommend to the school whether or not they should try to develop a partnership with the primary school in Lamin Darboe's village. They answered children's questions and, through their geographical enthusiasm, initiated ongoing discussion and generated curiosity and interest in the Gambia. The work was visual, oral and inclusive, with no writing. The partnership link has been established, the children and their teachers are seeking to develop mutual understanding of, and respect for, each other, their cultures, their schools and their countries.

The children in Case study 6.1 were using their graphicacy and oracy skills, and lots of speaking and listening to learn about the life of a family in the Gambia. They used artefacts, video and photographs and 'read' these as alternative texts. They used a globe, atlas and Google Earth to locate the continent, country and village. There was no written evidence for assessment, just the children's enthusiastic conversation, communication with the whole school through role play and recounting what they had learned to everyone who asked about it. And, most importantly, throughout all the activity, they were thinking and learning geography.

Innovative and creative approaches to geography

Geography is a visual subject, dependent on images. These may be first-hand in the urban or rural environment, townscapes or landscapes. They may be secondary sources like artefacts, videos, photographs, diagrams and maps of all sorts. But children cannot automatically 'read' these. They need to learn, through repeated encounters, how to 'see', interpret and understand them. And they enjoy doing it.

The combined Key Stages 1 and 2 case study described above used artefacts, three-dimensional objects that are part of what I like to call the *graphicacy continuum*. Graphicacy is the essentially pictorial communication of spatial or geographical information. It builds on visual literacy skills. In the case study the artefacts are visual and help to communicate something of the way of life in the Gambia, more specifically in a Gambian village compound. I wish the term 'graphicacy' were more widely used in geographical literature rather than 'mapwork'. I think it is more helpful and, to many non-specialists, less threatening. My experience suggests that many non-specialists give up on geography at the mention of maps, so low is their confidence in handling, let alone teaching about, them. The graphicacy continuum (Table 6.1) includes all the visual images available to the teacher to communicate geography with enthusiasm and to enthuse the learner.

Table 6.1 A checklist of the visual resources you can use in the classroom

Visual image	Examples
Fieldwork	The real world, a real joy and the ideal way of teaching and learning geography, from immediately outside the classroom to further afield, from ground level and higher perspectives, looking down on their world.
Artefacts	Three-dimensional visual images that children enjoy handling and talking about, and which can tell them much about places, cultures, ways of life.
Eye-level views	Children's most usual perspective on their world, familiar view of photographs.
Low- to high-angle oblique view	Looking at images taken from upstairs windows, tall buildings, from low- to high-flying aircraft – many photographs, postcards and, increasingly, books show these perspectives.
Oblique view pictorial maps	Many commercial maps today, especially for tourist attractions, parish maps and city maps, are pictorial and show a place from an elevated angle. They make a vital link between photograph and map.
Aerial, vertical view, photographs	Available commercially, especially from Wildgoose, and on the internet and Google Earth.
Maps of all sorts – vertical 'bird's eye' view	Street maps, road atlases, world atlases and, last but not least, OS maps of all scales.
3-D vertical view	Globes, both physical and political. Children should be helped to develop a virtual globe in their head so that when they learn about a new place or hear about a country on the media they can rotate their virtual globe and locate it. This comes, across the curriculum, with handling globes for places as much as they handle a dictionary for words.
Google Earth	A fantastic resource that can become obsessive – I know! – but children need a globe to handle alongside it to know which way to manipulate the image. They need to rotate a real globe before, or as, they rotate a virtual, flat-screen one.

Let me explain why I think the graphicacy continuum is so important. Apart from the pleasure I know children get from learning from fieldwork or secondary visual images, my main reason is to do with maps and mapwork. Experience and discussion with trainee teachers, many of whom fear or even hate maps, tells me that we rush into maps and the 'bird's eye view' with children far too quickly. And with the 90 degree angle between their usual, familiar view of the world around them and the vertical view, it is a huge conceptual leap. We wouldn't dream of making such a leap in any other subject, especially in literacy – to be expected to read a 'chapter' book as soon as we've grasped phonics – or in numeracy – to be presented with long division sums as soon as we can count. I don't think it is surprising that many children and teachers do not like maps. They need help in bridging the conceptual gap, and visual images of all sorts, from all angles, facilitate this. Many maps are things of such beauty that they deserve to be appreciated and enjoyed, not feared. Much of this is summarised in Figure 6.1 (Mackintosh, 2006).

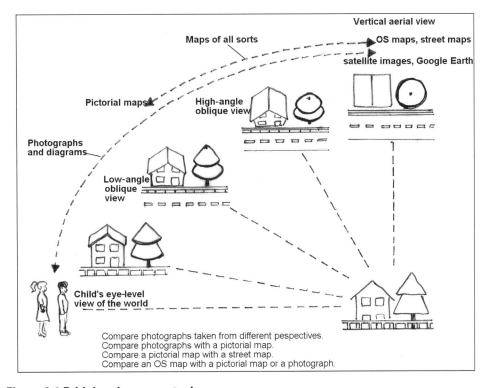

Figure 6.1 Bridging the conceptual gap

But using a graphicacy approach is not a complete panacea for joyful geography. Equally important is how the children engage with the visual images. My answer is using an *oral approach*, children being encouraged to talk to each other throughout their geographical activities as you listen in to their geographical conversation and engage in dialogue and questioning with them. This is enjoyable for them and makes you a creative and innovative geography teacher. Case study 6.2 gives you an example from a Year 6 class.

CASE STUDY 6.2

A different approach

The topic was Rivers, one which seems to put students off geography because they say they do it too many times in school. Many graphicacy resources were used. The class looked at a BBC video of the River Severn from source to mouth, a dynamic view of a river. They went on a field visit to the local River Otter, recognised features seen in the video and compared the Otter with the Severn.

Next, a set of ground-level photographs of the Otter from source to mouth were sequenced, to compare first- and second-hand experiences. This was followed by some aerial photographs and pictorial maps of the River Thames to interpret. Then the River Yangtze was introduced, with map, globe and Google Earth activities to locate it. From a river description read out by their teacher the children visualised the landscape and drew their own postcard from China. Finally the question was posed: 'Should the Three Gorges Dam be built?' This led to a role play or simulation activity which, with three children cooperating to play each interested party, became quite a heated debate as different angles on the issue were introduced and argued.

I have summarised this sequence because the key to its success, the amount that could be done in a limited time and the children's very active engagement with it was that there was *nothing to write*. The whole unit of work was oral and pictorial. Children's participation was not inhibited by their reading, writing or spelling ability. They could use the full extent of their geographical and other vocabularies. This approach, I know, raises questions about assessment and evidence, but while the children were eagerly involved in the activities their teacher was able to observe and listen in to their conversations, their use of key vocabulary and their questions. He was able to contribute to their discussions, extending their geographical thinking and posing his own questions to challenge them. This unthreatening situation, without the resort to literacy, led to high-quality geography being carried out enthusiastically. It also revealed some pleasant surprises, with children showing better levels of achievement and thinking than would otherwise have been possible. If you are able to work this way, ask yourself if anything is to be gained by the children writing things down, by recording things? If the answer if no, then don't make them do it.

You will probably find it helpful to have a transferable structure to your ongoing 'continuous' dialogue with the children while they work the way I am suggesting. The model is appropriate for all primary age groups. It follows the *observe* → *describe* → *compare* → *give reasons* → *explain* sequence, which is reflected in the geography level descriptions, if these are an important consideration for you. Much of this is summarised in Figure 6.2 (Mackintosh, 2006).

When you provide children with a geographical experience, fieldwork, video, artefact, photograph or map, for example, they will observe it. You need to discover what they are seeing, so ask them and they will describe it, orally. You will provide the words they lack. With this initial word bank they move from describing to comparing one example with another – pictures of the same locality or of two different localities. You will supplement their vocabulary whenever necessary. Doing this they will identify similarities and differences, or continuities and changes. When appropriate to their geographical progress they can try to give reasons for, or explain, their observations. This simple sequence develops geographical thinking and facilitates progress in a friendly, enjoyable way for teacher and learner. You will find that you very quickly internalise the stages in the sequence each child has reached and will have some pleasant surprises.

Unfortunately you might find it difficult to employ this approach in your school, as there may be pressure to write things down. But you are supported by the need to develop 'speaking and listening' in the curriculum, and the results will speak for themselves.

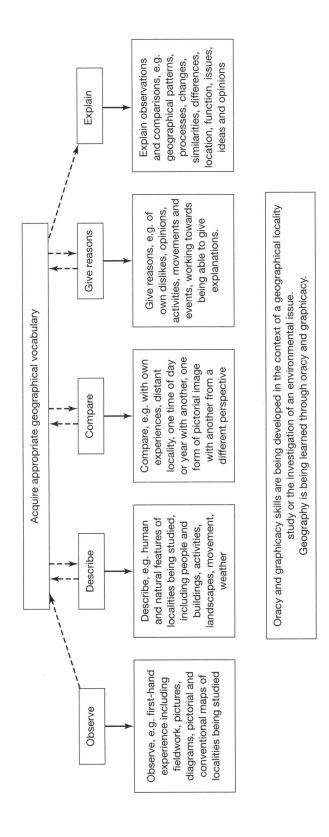

Figure 6.2 Progression in oracy in geography

Conclusion

In this chapter I have advocated a graphicacy and oracy approach to teaching geography which, I know from experience, is enjoyable for the teacher. There really isn't a need for children to write everything down for assessment, as the evidence can be pictorial and oral, using a teacher's professional judgement observing the children at work, eavesdropping on their conversations to hear their use of specific vocabulary as they work in pairs or small groups, and engaging in continuous dialogue with them. With a words and pictures approach you have got time to do this while the children are engaged in interesting and stimulating activities. Have the confidence to try it out.

To conclude I want to tell you about a learner, David. He was an eight-year-old boy in Year 3 who, despite having 'failed' at literacy and being assessed as having special educational needs, was having great success at geography and enjoying both the work and his achievement. This was because his teacher, Linda, was employing an oracy and graphicacy approach. She was teaching David to read a wide range of pictures and to talk about them with a partner and with her. She was using pictorial material as 'alterative text' and David was responding.

The pupils were studying their local area which, let's admit it, often elicits a groan of 'not again!' because they'd been bored by it on a previous, worksheet-led encounter. Linda had asked the school caretaker, on his weekly visit to the school roof to retrieve footballs, to carry a camera with him and take overlapping photographs of the school's surroundings in all directions. Pairs of children arranged the resulting low-angle oblique aerial photographs in sequence, discussing and matching landmarks to form a 360° ring centred on the school. David and his partner then placed a higher-angle oblique aerial photograph of the school in the centre and rotated it to coincide with their ring of photos by matching and comparing visual clues, using geographical vocabulary as they did this. They then orientated a large-scale OS map to relate to the photos in a similar way, and compared the aerial photo with the map by recognising similarities and identifying some differences or changes.

Linda provided each pupil, including David, with an A4 black and white photocopy of the aerial photograph. They each put it in a polypocket and, using dry-wipe pens, made a line drawing of the key features. They were learning, in the classroom, to make a field sketch. Removing the photograph, David placed his field sketch on an overhead projector (on the floor) and projected it onto a large sheet of paper pinned to the wall. He traced the projection, making a 'map', distorted a bit by the oblique angle of the photograph. At this point I had a conversation with David about his work. He told me about it with great enthusiasm. He said that when he went home he was going to go around the streets and write down their names so he could put this information on his map. He had created a need to write and collect data. Asked if he was enjoying this work he replied 'Oh yes, I can do pictures!' It was a cry from the heart. What he could also do, what he could also achieve success in, and enthuse about, was geography.

In these activities David had talked geography throughout, learned to 'read' both low- and higher-angle oblique aerial photographs and a 1:1250 OS map, compared and matched them, made a field sketch, used this to create his own 'map' and collected information to add to the map. Quite an achievement, especially for a boy labelled as having special educational needs. Much of his success, I am sure, was because he had not been required to write everything down on worksheets. And an approach that is appropriate for, and enthuses, a boy like David is appropriate for all the children in your class.

Further reading

Alcock, K. (2000) *Our World*. Dunstable: Folens/Belair.
This is a beautifully illustrated and inspiring book with classroom examples of Foundation Stage geographical work.

De Boo, M. (ed.) (2004) *The Early Years Handbook*. Sheffield: Geographical Association for the Curriculum Partnership.
Through twelve illustrated thematic case studies, this handbook helps Early Years practitioners provide fun and stimulating experiences that include geographical elements of the early learning goals.

Scoffham, S. (2005) *Primary Geography Handbook*. Sheffield: Geographical Association.
This handbook written by primary geography experts gives teachers the solid foundation they need to teach geography confidently, whether or not they have a background in geography.

References

Department for International Development (DFID) (2005) *Developing the Global Dimension in the School Curriculum*. Glasgow: DFID.
Hoffman, M. (1995) *Grace and Family*. London: Frances Lincoln.
Mackintosh, M. (2004) Talk and pictures in KS2 geography. *Primary English Magazine*, 10 (1), 23–7.
Mackintosh, M. (2006) Graphicacy: a vital skill. *Primary English Magazine*, 11 (4), 10–13.
North, W. (2006) The PG interview: Wendy North. *Primary Geographer*, 61, 21.
Owens, P. (2006) The PG interview: Paula Owens. *Primary Geographer*, 61, 12.
Palfrey, D. (2006) Taking a different view. *Primary Geographer*, 61, 32–4.

7
Enjoying teaching and learning outside the classroom

Sue Waite and Tony Rea

Introduction

Anyone who has stood at the doorway leading from school to playground will be in no doubt about the sheer joy and exuberance that erupts as children cross that threshold. Is it simply because play awaits or is there something more about being outside the four walls of the classroom that introduces possibilities for injecting joy into learning too? Adult memories of significant events from childhood often include references to the outdoors, so clearly something about being outdoors makes them memorable. This continuing pleasure in being outside is set in a culture where boundaries for children have become increasingly circumscribed by fears for safety. At the same time concern is growing about childhood obesity and fitness levels.

But is it all unalloyed joy? You may be aware of some children who will find any excuse not to go outside, exercise or get dirty. Our culture of fear and restriction may already have produced children for whom the great outdoors is rather the great unknown and some adults may also be averse to getting cold or wet in the name of learning. However, this chapter may rekindle your basic instinct for learning outside the classroom. After all, it is only in the last two hundred years or so that it has become the norm to learn inside those funny confines called schools.

Background

Rickinson et al. (2004) provide a helpful categorisation of types of outdoor learning:

- **the use of school grounds;**
- **fieldwork;**
- **trips and visits;**
- **outdoor adventurous activities.**

In nineteenth-century Germany, Froebel founded nursery gardens where children were encouraged both to play and learn outside. Children in Froebel's 'Kindergarten' were given small plots of land to tend and nurture, and were encouraged to observe the growing plants, thus stimulating awareness of the natural world. They were also places where children would exercise and play using songs, dances and movement games to help develop healthy activity. In Britain a century later Isaacs recognised the power of gardens for developing both spiritual and scientific learning and McMillan advocated the use of small, natural outdoor spaces to promote the health of children from underprivileged urban environments (Garrick, 2004).

Froebel took children on excursions into the surrounding countryside, but urban environments also provide prime learning opportunities for children. Many subjects, for instance science, geography and art, have at their heart observations of the outside environment. Children have regularly been taken outside to learn about them. Visits may also be made from the school to museums, galleries and theatres, so expanding our definitions of teaching outside the classroom.

Outdoor adventurous activities include climbing on rocks or over obstacles, building dens, going on some kind of expedition, perhaps going in, on or near water, and working together in a team to solve problems in a physical, experiential way. Such activities have a long tradition in the British educational system. They have been influenced by Lord Baden-Powell, who founded the scouting movement, and the theories of Kurt Hahn, the originator of Outward Bound. Central to the thinking of Baden-Powell and Hahn is the idea that by experiencing challenge and overcoming it, character is developed. There is a lot of recent research that suggests properly planned and managed outdoor adventurous activities can encourage a growth in self-confidence and self-esteem (e.g. Rickinson et al., 2004). This is not to suggest that thrusting children into the mouths of raging storms on open mountainsides may boost their self-concept, rather that safely managed outdoor adventurous activities are certainly worth considering as an essential part of children's learning.

What can learning outside the classroom achieve?

There are four key words to consider.

1. **F**itness– bigger spaces mean that bigger movements are possible so exercise increases physical fitness, coordination and well-being.
2. **R**ealise – the natural world provides a real-life authenticity for learning and helps to embed decontextualised learning.
3. **E**xtend – subjects covered in class can be productively extended by trips which bring new insights and learning.
4. **E**nthuse – novelty, fresh air, space.

You may notice that the initial letters of these spell FREE. Teaching and learning outside the classroom can free you as teacher and your children to explore and learn in new ways. The following two case studies illustrate some of the potential of outdoor learning.

CASE STUDY 7.1

Natural observation

At the start of her lesson on the development of frogs, the teacher seems quite directive. She refers to a science book the class have looked at inside and uses closed questioning with definite 'right' answers in mind. However, after a while teacher and pupils relax into the informal context outside and the children themselves start to discover new features of the outdoor environment, talking to each other and speculating.

The teacher worries about her lack of subject knowledge but in fact the children learn about enquiry through their own questioning and notice details about their surroundings. She supports this form of learning by organising the children into three groups; two go off to look for other signs of change in the grounds and one stays with her looking at the frogspawn. They notice many other creatures and plants in the pond and are really engaged in the activity, clamouring round the edge, squatting, pointing. The other groups roam the area, looking closely at grass, hedgerows and trees. Some wander to the boundaries of the grounds but are soon brought back by the teacher's request to stay around the area near the pond, 'so I know you are safe'.

After they have all had a chance to look at the frogspawn, they gather round the teacher, share some of their discoveries and she gives out sketchbooks and pencils. They then spend ten minutes making sketches of what they have noticed. They really look carefully when doing the drawing, frequently checking the match between the object and their representation and, in doing so, they notice fine details. She selects some children to show what they have noticed among their everyday surroundings. These include:

Buds on a tree – 'They're feathery … pink … brown … opening … blossoms'. The teacher picks up on rich descriptive language and suggests they continue to observe them in coming weeks to check if their guesses are right.

Lichen – 'It's the tree's leaves from last year gone white and grey … there are tiny black speckles … I don't think it is part of the tree … There is some on my granddad's bench … Is it just on wood? … Oh look, there's more, higher up the tree; I wonder why … you can get it in all sorts of colours, yellow …'. Nobody knows what it is but discovering it and making guesses fascinates them.

The children are very interested in their environment; they are focused on looking for new things and use talking, looking, listening, recording and reflecting to make it a rich learning opportunity. The naming of things does not seem important to them, but *how* things are and *why* they are as they are stimulates lots of thinking. The open discussion and speculation gives the teacher many opportunities to assess their understanding.

Back inside the classroom, the children create pastel drawings from their careful sketches – beautifully observed and accurate in colours and detail, capturing their wonder in a fresh observation of features they walk past every day on their way to school.

The vignette in Case study 7.1 illustrates how many things can come out of the apparently simple and commonplace activity of looking in the school pond. More learning is achieved by creating a space for children's speculation than by restricting the lesson to a narrow focus on giving the children an opportunity to see first-hand what they have been looking at in books inside. The children show themselves to be acute observers both in the range of what they spot and the fine detail they notice; they show signs of hypothesis building; they record; they co-operate.

They also learn about keeping themselves safe in an outside environment. While the teacher had spoken about potential risks before they went outside, the need to be careful around the pond and to be aware of possible dangers from cars in the area they visited, she also included the children in assessing risks, for example by asking them why they should take care on a steep bank. This shared approach develops children's sense of acceptable risk. Having laid these foundations of safety awareness, the teacher could simply remind them of the need to 'know they are safe' to reawaken a sense of responsibility for themselves. The examples in Figure 7.1 illustrate the wide variety of outdoor learning opportunities that you may be able to access in a primary school.

Reception

- Adventure playground (daily for all years).

- Exploring mini-beasts' behaviour to see how far they roam.

- Playing with toys outside, painting with water, sand play.

- *'Squirrel moments'* – one teacher described how seeing squirrels through the window excited the children's interest. It has been adopted as a shorthand for seizing the moment to offer refreshment from the planned curriculum through the stimulus of the unexpected outside.

Key Stage 1

- Tadpoles and other pondlife.

- Planting bulbs and growing plants.

- Following a route around school using a map.

- Bug hunts in wooded area to find out about mini-beast habitats.

- Wooded area to do rubbings of bark and see colours of leaves.

- History - trips to museums and cathedral.

Key Stage 2

- Swimming (weekly).

- PE (weekly) – children making up games.

- History – town to draw houses.

- RE – chalking Rangoli (traditional Indian) patterns in the playground.

- Geography – map drawing, fieldwork.

- Art – large-scale natural installations and observational drawing.

- Sculpture garden visits and drawing as a form of recording on many trips regardless of subject focus.

- Maths – for example, measuring with wheels.

- Science, including:

  - camouflage experiments using coloured pipe cleaners in grass bank;

  - sundials with sticks and circles.

- Church – brass rubbings and quiet thoughts developing a sense of awe and spirituality.

- Residential – adventurous outdoor activities.

- Farm visits to see animals, face fears and increase self-confidence.

- Zoo – stimulating research into animals, habitats, countries.

- Environmental residential – increasing self-confidence, pleasure in the outdoors and environmental awareness.

- Seaside – enjoyment and appreciation of local features, the sea.

Figure 7.1 Examples of out-of-classroom opportunities in a primary school

TO THINK ABOUT
TO THINK ABOUT

- Outdoor teaching and learning can take many forms and have many purposes. There are some activities that can only take place outside. There are others which could be done inside but are *enhanced* by an outdoor context.

- When planning for outdoor learning you should create a match between purpose and activity but also be aware that many other aspects, in particular personal, social and health outcomes, may also be achieved.

- Child-led outdoor activities are powerful for developing critical thinking because there are tangible authentic problems to solve in a natural context.

CASE STUDY 7.2

Farm visit

The children are excited as they walk to the farm. The sun is beginning to set and they know that walking back along the narrow path across the moor, one behind the other, they will be in almost total darkness. But for now the farm visit occupies their thoughts. What will it be like? Their teacher, Mr Brennan has told them that they are going to see the lambing shed and Ted, the leader from the residential centre, only says: *You will have to wait and see*.

As they enter the yard Mr Brennan shakes hands with the farmer and quickly they go inside the shed. It is huge! And the noise is deafening, with two hundred bleating sheep penned along the far side of the shed, crammed together waiting to give birth. The farmer keeps a careful eye on them, watching for those that are ready then frantically bringing them out of the large pen. Closer to the children are individual ewes that have been penned off by the farmer as they are about to lamb.

Look, cries Sean, *this one is having its baby now*. The other children crowd round. Mr Brennan looks over their shoulders. Ted prefers to look away. After a struggle the lamb is born and the children watch enthralled as it tries to get to its feet. Two boys are mesmerised as the ewe, tired after her efforts, looks at the afterbirth. 'That's the yolk,' speculates Robert. The farmer comes around with an antiseptic to put onto the open wound that was the umbilical cord. He picks up another lamb and lets the children hold it if they want to – not for too long, as the mother may yet reject it. In the corner behind them are a ewe and two lambs that did not survive the birth. The children don't notice this yet, but later a few will. There is a lot for Mr Brennan to follow up back at school.

As the group walk back to the centre Mr Brennan is talking to Ted: *You know, it's this they will remember. Not the end-of-key stage tests or the literacy hour. The children come back to visit us years after they have left the school, and it's their visit to the centre that they want to talk about*.

What children learn may be more than what is planned for them (see Figure 7.2). For example, the literature suggests evidence of powerful opportunities for spiritual development (e.g. Rea, 2003), especially in developing a sense of awe and wonder provided by outdoor environments. Though it does not appear in the centre's learning outcomes there is evidence to suggest it is occurring informally. Some children found the visit to the lambing barn awe-inspiring and talked about it at length afterwards. Walking over the moor at night allowed children to experience natural darkness, often for the first time, and research suggests transcendental experience is more common outdoors and in the dark (Paffard, 1973).

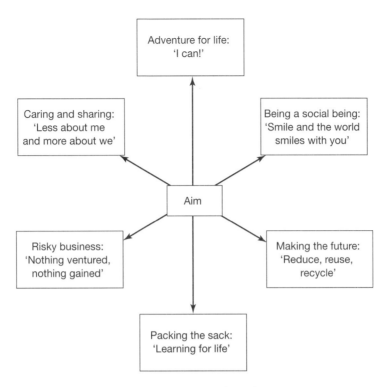

Figure 7.2 The aims of one residential outdoor education centre

Making use of the outdoor environment

Some residential centres encourage the children to play an active part in their efforts to operate on a sustainable and ecologically sound basis. Local wildlife experts may visit the centre bringing along animals like owls, stick insects and otters. But few activities take place indoors. The extensive natural grounds and surrounding area are used as an 'outdoor classroom'.

Other activities commonly offered include on-site activities, such as orienteering, a low ropes course and zip wire, problem-solving games, an obstacle course, climbing wall and poles. In the surrounding countryside and coast, surfing, canoeing, coasteering, beach survival, moorland walking and river studies are possible. Activities are not all physical. Staff from the centre encourage beach sculpting during a coasteering activity. They allow the children to use their imagination to create sculptures from natural materials. They take time to pause and encourage the children to observe and think about the land and seascapes around them, offering opportunity for feelings of awe and wonder.

Some schools choose to undertake specific studies that link with their school-based work and have an intended outcome that has direct links with the National Curriculum. For example, a walk along a local river offers opportunities to study river development in general as well as the natural history of a particular river that is prone to flooding.

Overcoming difficulties presented by the weather is embedded in the principles espoused by outdoor centres. Many centres purchase good quality waterproof coats, trousers, Wellington boots and rucksacks for all participants. The children are provided with a comprehensive kit list that includes warm socks, pullovers or fleeces, hats and gloves.

However, the children may have to live with some of the consequences, such as being cold or wet, if they do not take notice of the leader's advice – a valuable lesson in listening.

A washing and drying facility means that the children never need start a day's activity with wet gear. Similarly, the centres provide wet suits, rash vests, booties, caps and buoyancy aids when using the sea, thus ensuring that the weather rarely inhibits planned activities.

TO THINK ABOUT

- Visits to outdoor environments are memorable events in children's lives.

- There are numerous curricular links to be made.

- Staff at the centre will do much of the work for you (but not all of it).

- Spiritual learning through awe and wonder develops well in the outdoors.

- There's no such thing as bad weather, just bad clothing.

The outdoors and the curriculum

Some teachers worry that taking children out of school reduces the time for National Curriculum work. However, it is possible to teach huge sections of the National Curriculum through well-planned use of the outdoors. A project in Kent (Dismore and Bailey, 2005) involved Year 6 children at an activity centre where outdoor learning focused on specific aspects of the National Curriculum. The maths *Make It Count!* project stimulated children's mathematical understanding through raft building and testing, and maths-based initiative games. *Read All About It!* was a reading comprehension exercise conducted through a detective game and teambuilding games. Writing skills through *Write On!* were encouraged and structured through wall climbing, archery and initiative games. It is claimed that pupils who had previously been underachieving made significant progress in their maths, reading and writing through this approach.

The outdoors offers plenty of other opportunities for addressing and enriching the National Curriculum through cross-curricular links. Science and geography can be taught experientially through fieldwork: examples of activities include pond or rock pool dipping, river studies, visits to zoos or gardens, and making maps of the local area. There are reports that children learn such things better outdoors through structured fieldwork than in the classroom (Nundy, 1999). Similarly, history can be taught through educational visits, either to the locality, exploring the concept of history around us, or to historical buildings, castles, houses and monuments, or to a museum.

ACTION POINTS ACTION POINTS ACTION POINTS ACTION POINTS ACTION POINTS

> Identify outdoor spaces you will use – remember that the school grounds may be ideal.

> Select curriculum-related learning objectives and link these to appropriate activities including lots of movement to burn off calories.

> Do the risk assessment – or better still, get the children to do it with you.

> Enjoy the experience.

Being healthy

Children's health is emphasised strongly in the Every Child Matters agenda, and activity in the outdoors can play an important part in this process. In Britain and many other developed societies children spend a worrying amount of time indoors and inactive. There are many reasons for this: the widespread availability of TV and computerised entertainment; the growing use of cars to move children around; the perceived fear (by adults) of dangers associated with allowing children to play outside. There is evidence that such inactivity is leading to a growing number of children who are overweight, even obese, and that this is causing health problems.

While outdoor learning is not the antidote to all the ills in society, it makes a vital contribution to children's health. Activity in outdoor environments can take many forms: walking around a town to gather data for a project; doing orienteering to practise skills; a treasure hunt that involves careful reading of cryptic clues; problem-solving games that encourage thinking skills. All involve good exercise. For example, the children who had a good, long walk to and from the farm mentioned earlier returned having burnt calories and breathed lungsful of fresh air; they had worked up an appetite for a hearty supper and, once they had finished chattering about the new born lambs, slept soundly.

Managing risk

Another of the desired outcomes from Every Child Matters is 'staying safe'. No one would wish to argue with that, would they? But how do we keep children safe? Is it by restricting their exposure to risk or by managing that risk so they learn how to assess and manage it for themselves? Does removing risk also not tend to dilute challenge and excitement, qualities which children really value in their learning? The case studies above give some examples of the way in which challenge plays a part in the attraction of the outdoors for children. It could be argued too that learning cannot take place without an element of challenge. Learning is about extending from what is already known and moving beyond one's comfort zone.

Introducing challenge

The outdoors has special qualities which make it challenging; it is much more unpredictable than a classroom. Working out how to get around those factors is an opportunity to learn and problem solve, not just for children but for teachers. For example, what do you do if it is raining during your outdoor lesson? Here is your chance to think of lots of teaching ideas that rely on rain. How much is it raining? In what ways could children measure this? What materials are waterproof?

Children enjoy flexible resources so that activities extend as their capabilities change. Have you ever watched a toddler climbing up a slide? They may be just trying to make the task more challenging once they have mastered the 'climb to the top of the stairs and sit on your bottom' part. Getting children involved in deciding what sort of outdoor resources supports their learning and allowing them to think up new ways to use outdoor equipment is a good way to tap into their creativity.

ACTION POINTS ACTION POINTS ACTION POINTS ACTION POINTS ACTION POINTS

> Involve the children in designing outdoor areas and planning outdoor activities.

> Challenge them to find different ways of using equipment or spaces, say moving over the adventure playground by not touching the ground, or in a wood by building a den.

> Encourage the children to be involved in sharing responsibility for themselves and others.

Supporting creativity and spirituality

We know that the outdoors has long been the inspiration for artists, poets and novelists, so why not expose children to the wonders of the natural world to inspire them? In the example mentioned earlier, one teacher spoke of 'squirrel moments' when the chance sighting of a natural creature provided a catalyst for creative teaching and learning. Another class had spotted a hedgehog scuttling along the fence outside. This led to discussion of hedgehogs' lives and diet, a re-reading of *The Hodgeheg* by Dick King-Smith, with opportunities for personal and social education in talking about making mistakes, and creative writing. Seizing such moments injects novelty and excitement into what are often now tightly timetabled schooldays. Case study 7.1 (earlier) illustrated how the quality of artwork using traditional art materials can be enhanced by close observation of nature. Natural materials can also inspire large-scale artwork outside.

'Forest school' sessions take place in wooded areas and aim to improve self-confidence through chunking activities into small achievable steps and establishing strong positive relationships (Swarbrick et al., 2004). The construction of mini dens for 'forest friends' made out of a whittled length of wood and bits of wool and leaves can lead children to engage in extended storying and role play games. 'Forest school' works within Maslow's hierarchy (1943) so that basic needs to be fed, clothed and watered, to feel safe and to feel love and belonging provide a necessary foundation for motivation to achieve and be valued, to explore and understand and ultimately to be creatively, intellectually and spiritually fulfilled (see Figure 7.3).

Figure 7.3 A hierarchy of needs (adapted from Maslow, 1943)

Inspiring awe and wonder is a major contribution that the outdoors can make to supporting spirituality and many writers have attested to how the outdoors has special power to instil wonder (Rea, 2003). It can be found in the sense of something much bigger and more potent than us such as the sea crashing onto the shore or in the wonder of small things like tiny shoots pushing through the earth. Natural contexts also have the ability to calm and soothe troubled minds. Spiritual effects have been observed in midnight walks on residential trips when fear and excitement combine into enduring personal memories. Weather and the changing seasons are a rich resource for teaching children about our place in the world and how our existence is interrelated with all living things.

Creating space for spirituality

- Remember that learning outdoors is not just about space to be loud and make bigger movements; it can also be about being very quiet, listening for all the sounds that fill the 'silence' outside.
- Studying nature can be a good introduction to children thinking about spirituality and environmental responsibility.
- Speculating about why natural things are as they are not only opens up a window on children's scientific misconceptions but also on their worldview.

Conclusion

But what about those unenthusiastic souls we mentioned at the beginning of the chapter? Their ambivalence and the importance of perseverance even in the face of such reluctance may be explained in Kurt Hahn's words.

> *I once asked a boy who, on a sailing expedition round the Orkneys had encountered three gales, 'How did you enjoy yourself?' His answer was, 'Magnificently, except at the time.'* (Hahn, 1960, p5)

There are so many possibilities with learning outside the classroom that you will find numerous opportunities to include this vital aspect of teaching and learning in your own practice. Familiarise yourself with the school and local authority policies on taking children outside. Take account of the following issues:

- getting permissions from parents and the head teacher and carrying out a risk assessment of the venue;
- planning trips well in advance, preparing children for the visit and following up afterwards;
- spoiling the experiential spirit of novelty and excitement by over-preparation;
- planning activities to address the learning objectives you want to cover;
- allowing space for children to investigate by themselves, guided by their own interests.

Not all learning outside the classroom needs this level of forward planning. As we have discussed in this chapter, many benefits accrue from small-scale extensions into the outside space. Children and the teacher can be refreshed by serendipitous events and by approaching learning outside the classroom as a chance to use more experiential teaching techniques. Look for these opportunities and seize them!

Key Quote

It would not be too bold to assert that direct and indirect experience of nature has been and may possibly remain a critical component in human, physical, emotional, intellectual, and even moral development. (Kahn and Kellert, 2004, pvii)

Further reading

Balazik, D. (2006) *Outdoor and Adventurous Activities KS2/3 Lesson Plans*. London: A. & C. Black. Many useful ideas for activities with lesson plans for your adaptation and advice about planning trips and visits.

Barnes, P. and Sharp, B. (2004) *RHP Companion to Outdoor Education.* Lyme Regis: Russell House Publishing.
A comprehensive and well balanced resource mainly focused on outdoor education beyond the school environment.

Garrick, R. (2004) *Playing Outdoors in the Early Years*. London: Continuum.
Excellent historical background to outdoor learning with case study exemplars especially targeted at Early Years practitioners.

References

Dismore, H. and Bailey, R. (2005) If only: outdoor and adventurous activities and generalised academic development. *Journal of Adventure Education and Outdoor Learning*, 5 (1), 9–20.

Kahn, P.H. and Kellert S.R. (eds) (2004) *Children and Nature: Psychological, Sociocultural and Evolutionary Investigations*. London: MIT.

King-Smith, D. (1987) *The Hodgeheg*. London: Hamish Hamilton.

Maslow, A. H. (1943) A theory of human motivation. *Psychological Review*, 50, 370–96.

Nundy, S. (1999) The fieldwork effect: the role and impact of fieldwork in the upper primary school. *International Research in Geographical and Environmental Education,* 8 (2), 190–8.

Paffard, M. (1973) *Inglorious Wordsworths*. London: Hodder & Stoughton.

Rea, T. (2003) Why the outdoors may be an effective repository for spiritual development. *Horizons*, 23 (Summer), 12–14.

Rickinson, M., Dillon, J., Teamey, K., Morris, M., Choi, M.Y. and Sanders, D. (2004) *A Review of Research on Outdoor Learning*. Shrewsbury: NFER/Field Studies Council.

Swarbrick, N., Eastwood, G. and Tutton, K. (2004) Self-esteem and successful interaction as part of the forest school project. *Support for Learning*, 19 (3), 142–6.

8
Running, leaping and dancing for joy
Emma Sime and Denis Hayes

Introduction

Think back to your early school days. What are your most memorable moments in physical education? Maybe you are recalling with pride the moment when you swam your first stroke, or remembering the excitement of winning the egg and spoon race at the annual sports day. On the other hand you may well be already breaking out into a sweat as you recall a warm summer day playing rounders and, as if in slow motion, you replay the moment in your mind when all your class mates watched in anticipation as the ball flew through the air to your eager, awaiting hands, only for you to completely misjudge the distance, stumble on a clump of thick grass and look up to see the ball thud to the floor centimetres away from you.

Love it or loath it, there can be no doubt that physical education (PE) is unique, both in the demands it places on you the teacher and the movement experiences it provides for the children in your care. These movement experiences are of fundamental importance to each child's development and education and can have a major influence on an individual's future participation in, and enjoyment of, physical activity.

Through reading this chapter you will come to realise that your experiences of physical education, whether they be positive or negative, will have shaped you as a teacher of the subject. We suggest that the joy of teaching PE is to witness even the most unlikely child succeeding and growing, not just physically, but cognitively, socially and emotionally. You can find great delight, too, in recognising that as a teacher you have the potential and opportunity to make these experiences happy, exciting and stimulating.

Child and school cultures

Young children love to move, run, jump and be physically active. They spend many a happy hour rolling around the floor with their friends, dancing to their favourite tune, running and jumping, climbing on furniture, and all the time exploring the limitations and capabilities of their bodies – and of course driving their parents to despair. However, Doherty and Bailey (2003) warn of a conflict as children begin their school career and move from a 'child culture' that is represented by movement and action to a 'school culture'. Child culture tends to be associated with the following aspects:

- play;
- being in;
- physical proximity;
- testing own limits;
- the unexpected;
- sensory;
- physical development;
- I move and I learn!

On the other hand, school culture tends to be associated with the following:

- study;
- reading about;
- physical distance;
- respecting boundaries set by others;
- the expected;
- intellectual;
- physical inactivity;
- sitting still!

(Based on Doherty and Bailey, 2003, p3.)

The child culture and school culture elements provide a useful contrast:

- play: study;
- being in: reading about;
- physical proximity: physical distance;
- testing own limits: respecting boundaries set by others;
- the unexpected: the expected;
- physical development: physical inactivity;
- sensory: intellectual;
- I move and I learn!: sitting still!

The emphasis in a child culture is towards play rather than study, though there are many types of play and you have to make decisions about the extent to which you initiate the play or stand back and allow it to happen spontaneously. Similarly, a child culture necessitates children being closely involved (physically and emotionally) in what they are doing and not mere spectators. On the other hand, children learn by observing experts and from one another as they collaborate and explore their environment.

Most children enter the Foundation Stage still in touch with their 'child culture' and a desire to play, be active and explore with their bodies. As they progress into Key Stage 1 it could be argued that while other subjects are sedentary in nature and require children to develop a certain amount of restraint, PE is sensitive to the 'child culture'. Indeed, Wright (2004) believes that this is an expectation of the physical education curriculum:

> With very young children, where gaining mastery of movement is very much part of their social play, one would expect play values to be emphasised strongly in the primary physical education school curriculum. (p158)

Therefore, *if taught well*, physical education should be an area of the curriculum that children of all ages often find joyful; after all, many of the skills practised in PE are introduced through the medium of play, which is associated with feelings of joy and pleasure (Bailey, 2000).

Child-centredness allows for the fact that children will wish to test boundaries but, as the responsible teacher, you have to ensure that health and safety issues are taken into account when planning lessons. In this regard it is important to distinguish between 'liberation' (making sensible choices) and 'licence' (making reckless choices). Freedom to choose methods and strategies has to take account of overruling factors, such as safety and security, respect for feelings, availability of resources and time constraints. As teacher, you must ensure that the children are not only aware of the 'what' but of the 'why'.

Sometimes, explanations about (for example) the need to avoid transgressing another child's space and 'thinking first' are better explored initially in the classroom and reinforced in the large space. While it is good for children to delight in the unexpected, it is also important to provide the security that comes from intellectual engagement with processes and procedures, such as orderliness of equipment. It is one thing to tell pupils to stack the gymnastic mats and benches away tidily, it is quite another to explain the possible consequences of failing to do so.

The child-centred approach described by Doherty and Bailey (2003) is, of course, only a model, but a glance at the list (on page 64) elucidates the key principle, namely that the best practice of a child-centred approach to physical education must be integrated with curriculum requirements, the expectations of colleagues and parents, and safety considerations. Too much of a child-centred approach can lead to fun but little learning; too little results in a dull session in which children are so constrained that they lose the desire to learn and participate.

CASE STUDY 8.1

P.E.

Ian had never particularly liked PE and today's lesson was to be no exception. After the usual furore of changing and the excited chatter of those around him he began the long walk to the hall. Despite having done this short journey hundreds of times since starting at the school he still began to feel anxious about what lay ahead. He knew why he felt this way but unfortunately he felt unable to do anything about it; he just felt more comfortable when he was in his classroom.

As always, the lesson was characterised by a high level of imposed discipline and inactivity, with children sitting, waiting restlessly for their turn. Activities were either too easy, resulting in boredom, or too hard, resulting in disappointment and a teacher counting the minutes until the 'endurance test' was over. For a long time as a child Ian had done all he could to avoid PE lessons, hoping that the assembly would overrun or that another school event would take priority. Fifteen years later Ian was a qualified teacher and teaching PE …

Five-year-old Jack in Ian's class had looked forward to going into the school hall and doing PE. At home he loved running and would often beat his older brother in races. The pleasure that he felt when charging about, whirling his arms and shouting joyfully was unbounded. Jack's favourite game was 'chase', at which he was the undisputed master. Naturally the first time that Jack saw the wide open spaces of the hall and the climbing equipment spread across the floor he responded to his instincts and, whooping with delight, launched himself on the resources. Ian made his displeasure plain by banishing him to stand by the assistant at the side of the room. Jack soon learned that PE was a disciplined subject that required instant obedience and compliance. Lessons were slow-paced, precise and highly regulated. The children were given specific tasks to complete and, although Ian often expressed his satisfaction with the children's efforts, the tight constraints meant that Jack's enthusiasm gradually waned until his positive attitude deteriorated to one of resignation.

After the lesson had finished they filed back to the classroom and got changed. However, Jack's ordeal was far from over, for he had always struggled with getting dressed, especially doing up buttons. It wasn't that he was clumsy or lazy; the button just never seemed to be the right size for the hole and his fingers became numb from repeatedly trying to connect the two. He asked the assistant for help but she told him that he should know how to do buttons at his age, so he stopped asking and left his shirt and cuffs flapping loose. Ian chided him for being slow and untidy and pointed out that all the other children had tried hard to change quickly, so why couldn't he? Jack sighed and sat down, making little attempt to disguise his disappointment. He began to dream of wide open spaces and the freedom to run and run.

> Do not pass on your own negative experience of physical education – remember that you have the potential to make a difference to every child in your class.

> Aim for all of the children to be active for the majority of the lesson, while also ensuring that you allow time for them to evaluate their own and others' performance.

> Try to balance your concerns with regard to safety constraints with the need to allow children to explore and demonstrate their spontaneous enthusiasm.

Case study 8.1 shows clearly that joyful teaching and learning does not happen by chance; it relies in part on the choices you make as a teacher, which in turn depend on your own experiences, perceived competence and confidence in this area. Studies of physical education teachers have found that the way in which trainee teachers first learn an activity themselves determines how they teach it (Capel, 2005). This author also acknowledges that depth of knowledge influences pedagogical (teaching) choices and concludes that *how physical education is taught is as important as its content for pupils' learning* (p111). It would be fair to suggest then that those teachers who themselves had positive experiences as children are more likely to discover the joy of teaching PE and provide positive experiences for the children they teach.

This is not to say that if you are reading this and recalling your negative experiences that you are already doomed to continue this vicious cycle of being an uninspiring teacher of PE. However, if you were unfortunate enough to have an unsatisfactory time during your school days, you must be doubly vigilant in protecting your pupils from suffering in the same way. We hope that by reading this chapter you will begin to become more aware of the influence that your own education and your experiences as a trainee teacher have had on you and, through the process of reflection and critical analysis, encourage you to challenge some of the curriculum models and teaching strategies that you have experienced.

Learning to move

A word of warning then – if you find your self dreading your PE lesson and through lack of confidence and subject knowledge resorting to lessons like Ian's or subjecting your children *solely* to a whole-class game of rounders, football or any other team game without practising the necessary skills, think again! In discussions with many trainee teachers it is apparent that they find themselves reminiscing about their memories of such teaching and often recalling the inactivity and boredom that went along with it. They recall waiting for their turn to bat, making daisy chains, practising handstands on the periphery of the fielding area or doing just about anything other than becoming physically active. It is noticeable that it is usually the less able or less confident child who manages to 'hide' during these class games, not wanting to draw attention to themselves, afraid that the whole class may notice their inability in the public arena that uniquely characterises PE lessons. Physical education is concerned with fundamental motor skill development and should not focus on merely learning particular adult orientated sports; it is a *much* broader concept.

Children are not mini adults and you should avoid treating them as such, offering them diluted or 'top-down' versions of adult activities that do little to develop young children's movement, competence or self-concept, for by doing so you suppress their desire to learn and contribute and deny yourself the opportunity to discover the hidden riches of teaching PE. Rather, you should persevere to discover developmentally appropriate activities that encourage co-operation and avoid excessive competitiveness. Make it your aim to contribute towards, and not detract from children's growing contentment with this area of the curriculum as they move through the primary school and into secondary school.

The joy of teaching PE is in knowing that you have planned activities that are properly sequenced and suitable for pupils of that age and temperament, and observing every child experiencing an element of success. A child who is not taught the relevant skills at an appropriate age or is asked to attempt developmentally inappropriate tasks, e.g. asked to do a handstand without having first mastered taking weight on their hands in other ways, is unlikely to succeed and may perceive themselves as being 'useless at PE' and ultimately decide to stop trying. Conversely young children who learn the joy of movement, who enjoy physical activity and who have engaged in a variety of meaningful and empowering movement experiences are much more likely to be have developed a sense of physical competence and a positive attitude towards physical activity and therefore become active adults. At a time when obesity is viewed as a global epidemic and a contributing factor to serious ill-health, your success in developing positive attitudes in children could make all the difference to their future health and welfare.

The Every Child Matters (DfES, 2006) agenda emphasises the need to meet the needs of *all* children and you must therefore plan and organise learning experiences which take account of individual differences in their development. You may be asking: 'How do I know what is developmentally appropriate?' The best advice is to 'start with the child' and observe the children's *movements* during lessons as the first step to achieving this goal.

A 'child-centred' approach is not a recipe for ignorance; it requires a secure level of knowledge, skills and understanding on the part of the teacher. This foundation is important when teaching any subject, but arguably more so in the teaching of PE due to its transitory nature. Although every child is different and there is no such thing as the average child, and although their pace of development may differ, they will all pass through similar stages. Thus, Gallahue and Ozman (2003) provide us with pictorial representations of what a child may look like when performing various actions such as throwing, catching, running and jumping at various stages of development and go on to identify developmental difficulties that could assist the teacher in identifying where a child's difficulty may lie (see Further Reading at the end of the chapter). Another useful resource designed to promote high-quality observation, description and analysis of movement in order to develop the fundamental motor skills and raise standards for learners is the PEA UK CD-ROM *Observing Children Moving* (OCM). This interactive resource includes video clips of children performing a range of movements, i.e. rolling, jumping, catching and running, and has the potential to enhance a teacher's understanding of the development of fundamental motor skills and therefore promote high-quality movement education.

Once developed, these skills can be seen as the building blocks on which more complex skills can be developed. You should initially allow the children to practise their skills individually and then progress to working with a partner or in small groups. Not only does this ensure that all of the children are active, it also provides each child with a *greater opportunity for practice and improvement* (Bailey, 2000, p82). Innovative projects such as the Basic Moves Programme acknowledge that this crucial stage of development cannot be left to chance as *children's basic movement competence is the key to future participation* (Jess et al., 2004, p23).

The second case study epitomises the joy of teaching PE and it is wonderful to have been one of the group of teachers responsible for this magic moment.

CASE STUDY 8.2

Success at last!

Quite how Katie found herself where she was right now baffled her. Although she was in Year 6 at the time (aged 11 years) she was physically, socially and academically about three or four years behind her peers. Others, including her teacher, watching eagerly from the sidelines, believed in her. Her team mate who had passed her the ball believed in her. But it had taken until this moment for Katie to begin to believe in herself. Katie enjoyed PE lessons and knew that the other children were accepting of her limitations but she had not quite realised to what extent this was the case. Being picked to represent her class was the first stage in this realisation, as was the moment when she walked out onto the pitch for the school's first ever Tag Rugby Festival, made all the more special by the presence of the local professional rugby team and the local press.

There had been a real buzz around the place for the last couple of weeks as everyone had eagerly anticipated this day. Excitement was high. Katie had taken it all in her stride but now, at this crucial moment, panic began to set in. She could see the try line ahead of her and feel the cold wind on her face as she ran faster than she ever believed possible. 'Don't drop the ball, don't drop the ball', she repeated silently in her head, while all she could hear around her were the chants and cheers of her friends. 'Friends' — now that was a word she never thought she would hear herself thinking. 'Go, Katie, go!' they shouted in unison, willing her on to make the try line. Katie had heard about moments like this, where everything about you freezes and events go by as if in slow motion, but she never thought it could ever happen to her.

That moment of touching the ball to the floor will live with Katie forever, followed by the final whistle and her team mates running to congratulate her. It was the culmination of lots of hard work and was the crucial moment of acceptance in, what for Katie, had been a long journey.

TO THINK ABOUT
TO THINK ABOUT

- Katie did not reach this point by chance. It was the culmination of many years of teaching from practitioners who were committed to a physical education curriculum that focused on developmentally appropriate activities.

- Physical education can have a powerful and positive impact upon a child's self-concept, friendship patterns and the development of the whole child.

- Children, like Katie, who have learned appropriate motor skills, experienced success and discovered the joy of being physically active are more likely to become active as adults.

Conclusion

For many teachers the sheer pleasure of watching the children, red faced and breathless, bounding around the playground or school hall, clearly exhilarated by the opportunity to explore with their bodies, is unique, uplifting and truly joyful. However, many researchers into PE have warned against this 'busy, happy and good' approach. Through reading this chapter it has been our aim to share with you our belief that the real joy of teaching PE is seeing a child develop not just physically, but emotionally, socially and intellectually. Even if you harbour some doubts about your ability to teach the subject, you should be encouraged by the prospect of satisfied children, thriving on your teaching, proud of their achievements and going on to become healthy and active adults. Let them run, leap and dance for joy!

> **Key Quote**
> *To see young children growing in physical skills, self-confidence and self-worth is a truly enriching experience. Nowhere is it more visible than in PE.* (Duncan Goodhew, Olympic swimmer)

Further reading

Addy, L. (2006) *Get Physical: An Inclusive Therapeutic PE Programme to Develop Motor Skills*. Cambridge: LDA.
A useful resource that contains lesson ideas on how to develop the physical skills of all children aged 5–7, at the same time as addressing the needs of children with motor coordination difficulties.

Gallahue, D.L. and Ozmun, J.C. (2003) *Understanding Motor Development*. Madison, WI: Brown & Benchmark.
An easy to understand guide to motor development aimed at and with significant value for educators.

References

Almond, L. (1996) A new vision for physical education, in N. Armstrong (ed.) *New Directions in Physical Education*. London: Cassell, pp189–97.

Bailey, R. (2000) *Movement development and the primary school child*, in R. Bailey and T. Macfadyen (eds) *Teaching Physical Education*. London: Continuum, pp73–85.

Capel, S. (2005) Teachers, teaching and pedagogy in physical education, in K. Green and K. Hardman (eds) *Physical Education: Essential Issues*. London: Sage, pp111–27.

DfEE (1999) *National Curriculum 2000*. London: DfEE.

DfES (2006) *Every Child Matters*. London: DfES.

Doherty, J. and Bailey, R. (2003) *Supporting Physical Development and Physical Education in the Early Years*. Buckingham: Open University Press.

Jess, M., Dewar, K. and Fraser, G. (2003) Basic moves: developing a foundation for lifelong physical activity. *British Journal of Teaching Physical Education*, Summer, 23–7.

Wright, L.J.M. (2004) Preserving the value of happiness in primary school physical education. *Physical Education and Sport Pedagogy*, 9 (2), 149–63.

9
Enjoyment in the Early Years through critical reflection
Janet Rose

Introduction

Joyful teaching would seem to have a natural place in the Early Years environment. The particular context of young children embarking on their first years of schooling, open, fresh-faced and eager to apply their natural exploratory drive to learn, creates a positive and life-affirming environment for practitioners to operate within. Not only is this a highly significant period of development, it offers a natural and opportune context to create fun, stimulating and joyful learning experiences.

The intention here is not to document ways of ensuring effective provision for younger children. These have been successfully discussed elsewhere and readers are advised to consult the key texts listed at the end of this chapter. Instead, this chapter will focus attention on ways in which you can help to ensure your teaching is joyous for both yourself and the young children with whom you work.

A key theme that will be explored is how the role of critical reflection on practice can help to enthuse you to become an 'educational connoisseur' (Eisner, 1998). By careful examination of aspects of your teaching and clarification of ways in which you can improve the quality of your provision, you can ensure more effective as well as gratifying practice. In doing so, you can become a proactive change agent and self-determining practitioner of your own professional development. Case studies will be reviewed to illustrate the empowering process of active reflection that can help you to generate a fulfilling professional life and a joyful classroom. Before reviewing these case studies, some key points for consideration will be highlighted that demonstrate the pivotal role that your thoughts and emotions play in providing positive learning experiences.

Key Quote
It is what teachers think, what teachers believe and what teachers do at the level of the classroom that ultimately shapes the kind of learning that young people get. (Hargreaves, 1995, pvii)

The thinking teacher
Thinking lies at the heart of a good teacher

Teachers' thought processes play a substantial role in the educational process. Moyles et al. (2002) talk about how effective pedagogy in the early years encompasses *what practitioners do and think and the principles, theories, perceptions and challenges that inform and shape it* (p5). It has been shown how educational practice is ultimately based upon teachers' system of beliefs, values and principles that inform their decision-making. The composite professional knowledge or 'practical theory' that guides teachers' classroom decision-making appears to encompass far more than operational procedures and subject expertise. From the beginning, teachers enter the profession with a strong sense of personal identity and of personal values.

The work of Spodek and Saracho (1988) on the practical knowledge of early childhood practitioners also accentuates the value-driven nature of teachers' practical knowledge. They note a moral dimension within such knowledge, based upon differing notions of the good, the true and the beautiful, which cannot be derived from childhood development theory. The authors argue that the thought processes of early childhood teachers comprise both *scientific concepts* related to the processes of education (such as learning theories) and *value beliefs* which are concerned with the products of education and are based upon moral judgements and social expectations.

As a classroom practitioner, you need to question your personal practical knowledge base and expose unreflective, habitual ('taken for granted') practice. The aim is to move away from making 'practical provision' (things for children to do) to a consideration of the underlying values, beliefs, knowledge and understanding that directs your thinking and thereby your practice. There is also evidence of inconsistencies between *espoused beliefs* and *actual practice* which give further credence for teachers to examine the thinking behind their actions (Bennett et al., 1997; Rogers and Rose, 2007). You must learn to confront the assumptions and beliefs underlying your practice by constantly reviewing, renewing and reflecting on them (Hargreaves and Goodson, 1996).

The remainder of this chapter highlights the difference between pragmatic reflections on practice and a more intensive kind of critical reflection undertaken by the practitioners, as demonstrated by the case studies below. But first it is important to acknowledge the integral place of *emotions* in this process.

Key Quote

Pleasure, desire and emotions are powerful motivators of learning [which] drive our actions and interactions with others. (MacNaughton, 2003, p53)

Emotions lie at the heart of thinking

The importance of the affective dimension (associated with feelings) to the thinking process and the significance of 'emotional intelligence' is now widely recognised (Goleman, 1995). Emotional intelligence appears to play an important role in interpersonal relations and the conduct of socially appropriate behaviour, while different facets of the emotional state do appear to affect cognitive performance – the mental process by which knowledge is acquired – and the learning process. Emotions may also act as the main motivating force behind decision-making through arousing, sustaining and directing our activity because emotional signals focus our attention and give rise to conscious reflection (Oatley and Johnson-Laird, 1987). Consequently, without well developed emotional intelligence, decision-making can be seriously impaired, since most decisions adhere to a personal value system.

Nias (1993) highlights the deeply emotional relationship that teachers have with their work and explores some of the reasons why teaching is so highly charged with feeling. She suggests that the reasons lie with the nature of the teaching profession, since it involves intensive personal interactions and entails close, even intimate, contact with other human beings for whose conduct and progress teachers are held responsible. Furthermore, Nias argues that teachers invest their 'selves' in their work to the extent of *merging their sense of political and professional identity* (p297). Nias also draws attention to the extensive evidence that shows how the teaching profession is imbued with a strong 'commitment to caring'. As Fullan puts it, *teaching at its core is a moral enterprise. It is about making a difference in the lives of pupils* (1995, p253) and in some way making them better.

Edgington (2005) describes teaching in the early years as a joy and a challenge and says that many Early Years teachers feel passionate about their profession and their practice. She writes that *young children deserve to be surrounded by optimism and enthusiasm* (p8) and highlights research that demonstrates how children can rapidly become resentful and unhappy if their social and emotional needs are not met. Consequently, in planning an appropriate curriculum for Foundation Stage children you must consider the children's social, emotional and physical, as well as their intellectual, needs (QCA/DfES, 2000).

TO THINK ABOUT

It is emotional intelligence that helps to create the kind of disposition or 'critical spirit' necessary for you to undertake critical reflection on your practice. Such reflection can help to generate positive feelings within your sense of self, which has important repercussions for your sense of personal professional identity.

Key Quote

To be passionate about teaching is not only to express enthusiasm but also to enact it in a principled, values-led, intelligent way. (Day, 2004, p12)

Critical thinking lies at the heart of joyful teaching

The case studies that follow demonstrate how you can achieve a better understanding of existing educational provision and effect positive changes in practice through the adoption of critical reflection and action research. Action research is a method of looking more closely at a particular aspect of your practice by a process of systematic investigation. It stimulates you to consider the underlying values and assumptions that inform and influence practice, to question the effectiveness of professional actions and judgements and the impact these have on the children with whom you work. With action research, reflection becomes a more deliberate and conscious process and has a more proactive and practical agenda. This increased insight can lead you to make better evaluations and more appropriate decisions about learning, thereby transforming the quality of children's experiences.

In addition to improving provision, action research can play an important part in re-enthusing and re-empowering you, as these case studies will show. You can be made to feel more professionally alert and empowered to make significant changes in your professional life. You will see how action research can also increase your self-esteem and help to establish a long-term habit of self-examination. Brookfield (1987) has described the emotional impact of the 'assumption hunting' process:

> As we abandon assumptions that had been inhibiting our development, we experience a sense of liberation. As we realise that we have the power to change aspects of our lives, we are charged with excitement. As we realise these changes, we feel a pleasing sense of self-confidence. (p7)

A self-perpetuating cycle can be established in which action research stimulates critical reflection and gives an emotional boost, both of which enhance your professional self-respect. In turn, this empowers and motivates you to continue to employ a critical style of thinking in your practice.

Making your teaching joyful

The following sections outline some case study examples of Early Years teachers who have taken time to investigate their practice and reconsider their provision. They each undertook action research as part of an Early Childhood Education Research Project called the Principles into Practice Project (PiP Project) based in the London area in which over one hundred Early Years practitioners took part (Rose, 2001). All of them claimed powerful benefits for themselves and the children in their care.

The stories described below (all based on Rose, 2001) indicate how the teachers' investigations and crucial reflections on practice led to changes in their professional thinking, the generation of new understanding and the revision of habitualised practice. It enabled them to focus attention on the children beyond traditional assessments and helped to rekindle an interest in children's learning. They came to re-evaluate the stereotypical adult role and the way in which they related to the children, to reconceive their practice from the perspective of the children and their needs rather than from adult agendas, and to recognise their capacity to implement improvements and become agents of change.

The process imbued all the practitioners with a new sense of excitement and enjoyment in their practice. The new discoveries they made and the sense of fulfilment they acquired helped them to feel more in control of their practice which in turn often created euphoric feelings of accomplishment. In effect, it made these practitioners become more joyful.

TO THINK ABOUT

- Teachers' thinking has significant pedagogical consequences that affect children's learning.

- Teachers' thoughts are guided by their practical theory of teaching and underlying beliefs and principles.

- Teaching is an emotionally charged process and emotions are integral to the thinking process.

- Teachers need to systematically examine their thinking and actions through critically reflective research on practice.

- Critical reflection on practice is a powerful means of generating professional fulfilment and the creation of positive and beneficial learning experiences for pupils.

CASE STUDY 9.1

Appropriate intervention

Sarah is a Reception teacher who chose to investigate children's speaking and listening skills in the role play area with a particular interest in those she perceived to be reluctant speakers. Sarah chose to observe children in different circumstances from normal, such as in the role play area. This initiated an 'assumption hunting' process within her thinking. She talked about how she had found the research so rewarding in that you could find out so much about a child and that her findings were a revelation. The research served to demonstrate how Sarah's predictions of children's abilities were shown to be flawed. She noted how the research had:

made me aware of how easy it is, as a teacher, to underestimate the abilities and competencies of children who are reluctant speakers. It also has encouraged me to broaden my assessments of children's speaking – looking at more informal talk.

The results of Sarah's observations prompted the uprooting and reorganisation of ingrained presumptions about children's communicative skills and deep-rooted beliefs about the adult role. This led her to retranslate her overall conception of the adult role as she realised that:

teachers don't always have to interact with the child for the child to be learning or to be doing something of value. That sometimes sitting back and watching what the child is doing or learning from each other in some constructive play situation or even an unstructured one, one that they're structuring themselves, is of equal if not greater value than a teacher-led activity ... There's so much more to children's communication than just adult–child talk.

Sarah had always felt that

Intervention was something you feel you ought to do ... I felt pressured as a teacher to intervene and take the language onto a higher level.

Sarah considered that this action was what was expected of her and vocalised the sources of this pressure to intervene and be doing something to include parents, the head teacher, the school governing body and outside bodies like inspectors. The compulsion that Sarah felt was placed upon her by the wider society became a frequent topic of conversation. She often expressed frustration at the contradictory messages between the didactic (direct) teaching style she felt society expected of her and the interactive style of teaching that she preferred.

Sometimes intervention is not a good thing because the play or the talk that's going on stops because children want to make you happy and give you the answers that you want or what they think you want.

Sarah came to believe that she no longer had to perform in her customary role in order to maximise children's learning. Her case is interesting, not only because she learned important lessons about appropriate adult interaction but because she seems to have become consciously critical of the socially conventional power relationship between teacher and pupil. Her recognition of the untenable nature of the authoritarian teacher role and her consequent adjustments to the way in which she related to her pupils led her to embark upon a more egalitarian form of practice. Sarah noted:

I have seen how easy it is to intervene as an adult in the wrong way. I no longer feel guilty if I am in that area observing and not interacting. I need to observe before I can help the play.

Sarah came to learn that she did not have to conform to the typecast image of a teacher constantly instructing pupils and directing their learning. She came to develop a relationship with the children so that they could learn *with* rather than merely *from* their teacher.

CASE STUDY 9.2

Building blocks

Teachers Katharine and Eileen investigated block play in their nursery. They decided to look more closely at how the children used the large wooden blocks and their own role in planning for and participating in the play. The teachers were particularly interested in the children's use of blocks as a mathematical tool for learning. Previously they had just got the blocks out and left the children to build on their own. When they started observing the children's play they were surprised at the extensive range of learning the children were developing, particularly in terms of social skills and mathematical understanding. Not only did they look more closely at what the children were doing and how they were using the blocks, they also investigated whether their own comments and interactions helped or inhibited the children's development and enjoyment. They realised that they had underestimated the complexity of the learning the children were experiencing and realised the role that they could play in developing this.

Once they became more alert to how the children were using the blocks, the way they were co-operating and the mathematical language they were using, Katharine and Eileen become more aware of the various skills and concepts the children were developing and ways in which they could build upon and extend the children's learning. They discovered that increased adult interaction often helped to sustain activities with some children, particularly girls, that they could provide assistance with developing mathematical language and concepts, and that block play was an effective means of developing social skills, particularly co-operation. This in turn led to their greater participation in the block play acting as a co-player as well as a supporter and extender of learning. Katharine and Eileen also recognised the need to allow children time to explore and operate independently. As a result of their investigations and subsequent adaptations in their practice, these practitioners noticed that the children had

developed their thinking and understanding in the block play area. They use their imagination more to develop complex constructions and become much more spatially aware. There is much more co-operative play taking place. With adult intervention the children have begun using language to describe mathematical concepts – symmetry, balancing, size, measuring, predicting, estimating – and this has grown significantly. Girls continue to need support and space to develop their building but girls and boys have now begun to co-operate together in constructing.

Katharine and Eileen's new found awareness meant that, in their own words:

Now, no matter what's going on, you are always thinking of either encouraging their ideas and development or even just being aware of what they're doing over there [in the block area] ... Automatically you are just thinking all the time.

They also believed that the research:

enhanced the teamwork among the staff and increased our commitment to the values of block play as a way of developing children's social, imaginative and manipulative skills as well as mathematical concepts.

Moreover, their research helped them to feel excited, enthusiastic and motivated in their professional life.

CASE STUDY 9.3

Outdoor learning

Ann is a nursery teacher in a primary school. She had previously taught Reception age children but was relatively new to the situation. Ann chose to focus on the outdoor area as she felt this was an aspect of her practice that she needed to improve. She was aware that use of the outdoor area was limited to short periods of time and only when the weather was fine. Her investigations mainly revolved around experimenting with different types of outdoor equipment and spending time observing and photographing what the children were doing. Initially these observations merely revealed what she had seen them doing a hundred times before. It was only when she took time to reflect and discuss these observations from a different perspective (by looking at the actual learning that was taking place) that she found so much that revealed the tremendous amount of learning that was actually happening during these activities. These observations and her subsequent reflections upon them were enlightening in terms of realising what children were capable of doing, the learning potential offered by the outdoor area and her own role.

The research helped Ann to become conscious of the underlying learning skills and cognitive concepts that children could develop in this area, the value of the social interactions that occurred between them and the need to be more discriminatory in her own interventions. She noted that:

I used to intervene a lot and I've realised that sometimes it's more important to stand back and let them get on ... Just reflecting on what they've done, you can see they get other children to help them.

Ann recognised that she had developed an alternative way of thinking about her practice. She acknowledged that prior to the research she did not really know what she was doing. However, when she started in the nursery:

I regarded the outdoor area as being completely separate from the nursery classroom. It was where the children were to release some of their energy. It was just a matter of thinking: 'Right, I'll put this out today because I didn't have it out yesterday'. But now I know why I'm putting things out, why I'm choosing things. It's thinking, 'Why do I need to do this? Why do the children need this? If we do this, what will happen?' The way I approach the outdoor area now is totally different from what I used to do before.

The shift in Ann's thinking appears to have been more than the unearthing of a few assumptions. The underlying premise upon which she based her decision-making had shifted from superficial provision of learning activities to a more experimental and deeply questioning approach. This is indicative of a paradigm shift that included reassessments about her role as a teacher, the children's learning potential and the style of educational experiences she offered them, in which the processes rather than the products of learning now took prominence. Collectively these alterations in previously held beliefs, knowledge and values led to a comprehensive re-evaluation of the leading premises upon which she interpreted and promulgated her entire practice. The research led her to develop a sense of power and a belief that she could change what was going on for the better. Ann declared:

You are in charge of what you are doing and can change your practice at your own pace ... it encourages you to be more reflective about your practice rather than having change imposed on us and not understanding why.

TO THINK ABOUT
TO THINK ABOUT

- **What are your underlying beliefs and values about teaching and children?**

- **How do you conceive your role to be as a teacher?**

- **What kind of relationships do you want to establish with your pupils?**

- **What kind of role in children's play will you adopt?**

Key Quote
Effective teaching and learning relies, at its heart, on the exercise by teachers of sustained passion. (Day, 2005, p135)

ACTION POINTS ACTION POINTS ACTION POINTS ACTION POINTS ACTION POINTS

> **Do not neglect to 'teach' children in order to progress their learning, but ensure that your teaching approach is one that will be most effective and of most benefit for all children.**

Conclusion

The quality of the relationship between adults and pupils and the style of practice that practitioners adopt is vitally important, with potential consequences for any stage of children's development, although it has been given special emphasis within the literature on early learning. The majority of the work on child development and early education draws attention to the importance of learning provision that is child-constructed rather than simply teacher-imposed, that has a child-centred curriculum where 'finding out' is emphasised as much as 'being told', with children as active participants in their learning rather than mere recipients, and where teachers adopt an appropriate interventionist approach rather than one of interference in their interactions with children.

Indeed, the significance of the adult role in education cannot be stressed enough. The literature on children's development and the field of education in general makes continual reference to the importance of the quality of the relationship between teacher and learner. Above all, teaching is led by sensitivity to the learner, and the type of role and mode of interaction a teacher chooses to adopt has a crucial impact on children's learning. The work of Donaldson (1978) shows how dependent children are on the language and interactive style of the adult in learning perception and making sense of their experiences. Such attention to the teacher's role in the learning process and the interactive communication between teacher and child helps to counteract problems that may occur, such as different interpretations of the task. The quality of adult conversations with children is a particularly significant factor in promoting their development (Siraj-Blatchford and Sylva, 2004).

If you are to scaffold children's learning by providing appropriate resources, applying timely interventionist strategies and assessing children's proficiencies, you will need to have a conscious awareness of your own role and the consequences of your actions upon the educational process. By articulating your implicit ('inner') belief system, by carefully examining any pre-judgements made of children's aptitudes and by investigating the nature of your interactions, you are more likely to develop a pedagogic role that is finely tuned with children's developmental needs and encompasses more proactive expectations of children's learning potential.

The teachers in the case studies referred to in this chapter developed a more critically reflective approach to practice, which led them to undertake a more supportive and interactionist rather than didactic teaching style, to broaden their agenda to incorporate the child's perspective, to give prominence to the processes of learning as well as the products, and to appreciate the value of observations in revealing children's real capabilities instead of simply surmising them.

By investigating your own practice, you can become empowered to engender more worthwhile provision for the children in your care. It is clear from the case studies highlighted here that it is possible for you to be vitalised and enthused, to become more adventurous and more confident, to increase morale and self-esteem, to be more interested, positive and satisfied with your practice – to be, in effect, more joyful.

Further reading

Dowling, M. (2000) *Young Children's Personal, Social and Emotional Development*. London: Paul Chapman Publishing.
An invaluable insight into children's development and an excellent source of material for helping teachers to understand children's needs.

Edgington, M. (2005) *The Foundation Stage Teacher in Action*. London: Paul Chapman Publishing. Essential reading for Foundation Stage teachers, encompassing key aspects of effective pedagogy, policy matters and theoretical issues related to working with young children.

Willan, J., Parker-Rees, R. and Savage, J. (2004) *Early Childhood Studies: An Introduction to the Study of Children's Worlds and Children's Lives*. Exeter: Learning Matters.
A comprehensive overview of current issues relating to the field of early childhood studies that incorporates important social, cultural and developmental aspects of young children's lives.

References

Bennett, N., Wood, E. and Rogers, S. (1997) *Teaching Through Play: Teachers' Thinking and Classroom Practice*. Buckingham: Open University Press.

Brookfield, S. (1987) *Developing Critical Thinkers: Challenging Adults to Explore Alternative Ways of Thinking and Acting*. Buckingham: Open University Press.

Day, C. (2004) *A Passion for Teaching*. Abingdon: RoutledgeFalmer.

Donaldson, M. (1978) *Children's Minds*. London: Fontana.

Edgington, M. (2005) *The Foundation Stage Teacher in Action*. London: Paul Chapman Publishing.

Eisner, E.W. (1998) *The Enlightened Eye: Qualitative Inquiry and the Enhancement of Practice*. Englewood Cliffs, NJ: Prentice Hall.

Fullan, M.G. (1995) The limits and the potential of professional development, in T.R. Guskey and M. Huberman (eds) *Professional Development in Education: New Paradigms and Practices*. New York: Teachers College Press.

Goleman, D. (1995) *Emotional Intelligence: Why It Can Matter More than IQ.* New York: Bantam Books.

Hargreaves, A. (1995) Series Editor's Introduction, in J. Smyth (ed.) *Critical Discourses on Teacher Development*. London: Cassell.

Hargreaves, A. and Goodson, I. (1996) Teachers' professional lives: aspirations and actualities, in I.F. Goodson and A. Hargreaves (eds) *Teachers' Professional Lives*. Abingdon: Falmer.

MacNaughton, G. (2003) *Shaping Early Childhood: Learners, Curriculum, Context*. Buckingham: Open University Press.

Moyles, J., Adams, S. and Musgrove, A. (2002) *SPEEL Study of Pedagogical Effectiveness in Early Learning*, Research Report No. 363. London: DfES.

Nias, J. (1993) Primary teachers talking: a reflexive account of longitudinal research, in M. Hammersley (ed.) *Educational Research, Current Issues*. London: Paul Chapman Publishing.

Oatley, K. and Johnson-Laird, P.N. (1987) Towards a cognitive theory of emotions. *Cognition and Emotion*, 1 (1), 29–50

QCA/DfES (2000) *Curriculum Guidance for the Foundation Stage*. London: QCA/DfES.

Rogers, S. and Rose, J. (2007) Ready for Reception? The advantages and disadvantages of single-point entry to school. *Early Years*, 27 (1), 47–63.

Rose, J. (2001) The impact of action research on practitioners' thinking: a supporting case for action research as a method of professional development. Unpublished PhD thesis, London: Goldsmiths' College.

Siraj-Blatchford, I. and Sylva, K. (2004) Researching effective pedagogy in English pre-schools. *British Educational Research Journal*, 30 (5), 713–30.

Spodek, B. and Saracho, O.N. (1988) Professionalism in early childhood education, in B. Spodek, O.N. Saracho and D.L. Peters (eds) *Professionalism and the Early Childhood Practitioner*. New York: Teachers College Press.

10
The joyful teaching of reading
Arthur Shenton

Introduction

The subject of this chapter, which will focus on three case studies, will be the teaching of reading as a joyous experience for both teacher and learner. Walk into any high-street bookshop or library today and you will see that we are living in an age of great writing for children. Story writers such as David Almond, Roald Dahl, Anne Fine, Anthony Horowitz, Dick King-Smith, Jan Mark, Michael Morpurgo, Philip Pullman, J.K. Rowling and Jacqueline Wilson are just a few of my favourites weaving fabulous stories with their wonderful words. One of the most important aims for primary school teachers must be to open up this marvellous world of books and reading to the children they teach. We need to teach children to read but more than this we need to teach them to love reading so it becomes for them a lifetime's pleasure. Reading is one of the great pleasures in life for me and I have been an avid reader as long as I can remember. Where did my love of reading come from? It is a difficult question to answer but there is no doubt it was partly inspired by one of my primary school teachers described later in the chapter.

> **Key Quote**
>
> *Our aim is not to teach decoding or sounding out or recognising words. It is to instil a love, an attitude, a passion. Right from the beginning.* (Jennings, 2005, p7)

CASE STUDY 10.1

Can I read?

This case study starts at the beginning of that journey to become a lifelong reader. Riley (1999) states that young children have an *unshakeable belief that they too will be readers ... one day soon* (p29). Is this always the case? It did not apply to the child in the study and may not be true for all children, particularly if, like Edward, they have a special educational need.

Edward has autism. He is in a Year 1 class and he is supported by a one-to-one teaching assistant in a main-stream class. He has worked with her since he started school and they have developed a close working relationship. For Edward reading is a complete mystery. He watches the other children reading and enjoying books and wonders if he will ever master what appears to him to be a magical skill. He can recognise some letters as the class is using Letterland for phonics teaching and focuses on two letters each week. The class is also working on learning groups of high frequency words many of which have irregular spellings and could not be learnt phonetically. Edward has joined the rest of the class in learning his own small group of high frequency words – 'I', 'a' and 'am'. He is practising these regularly with his teaching assistant. One of my student teachers is working with this class on her school experience and has chosen Edward for the case study she is required to do focusing on his reading development.

When her school practice was finished she recounted to me a conversation she overheard between Edward and one of the other children in the class who had obviously mastered the art of reading which Edward felt was so beyond him. During independent learning, Edward turned to the boy next to him who was lost in the book he was reading and asked, *How do you read?*

His friend was uncertain how to answer because for him reading had become second nature, like breathing. *You just do it*, he said, rather dismissively turning back to his book.

I can't read, Edward commented with a resigned sigh.

The class teacher overheard the conversation and intervened. She went to the whiteboard and wrote the word 'am' – one of the high frequency words that Edward was learning. *What does that say Edward?* she asked.

Am, he replied.

The teacher smiled and nodded.

Is that it? said Edward. *Was that reading? Can I read?*

It was as if up until that moment Edward did not fully understand what reading was. Children with autism often find abstract concepts and language challenging but it seems that at that moment with the teacher's sensitive intervention building on the word work Edward had been doing with his classroom assistant, he began to see himself as a reader for the first time.

This realisation that he could read, even if it was only reading three words, made a huge difference to his confidence and motivation and my student teacher saw his interest in reading and reading activities blossom during the following weeks. He began to take an interest in words around the classroom, copying them into a little book he had been given and asking others what the word said. More importantly the student teacher described how the child began to find pleasure in reading and sharing books with her and his teaching assistant. During one particular week, she read a big book version of Jill Murphy's *Peace at Last* with the whole class adding percussion to the story during a music lesson. Edward loved the book, joining in with the rest of the class reciting the repeated elements. He saw himself integrated now into that 'reading club' he thought he would never be able to join. Skilful, sensitive teaching by teacher, teaching assistant and student teacher had allowed Edward to begin to see himself as someone who can now 'behave' like a real reader.

TO THINK ABOUT

- Children need to feel that they are not excluded from the 'reading club'. Sensitive teachers can make children believe they are part of this club even at the very early stages of learning to read.

- Confidence in reading builds children's self-esteem and can have positive effects across the curriculum.

- We must read to, and share books with, children even at the earliest stages of learning to read if we are to instil a love of books and reading.

Key Quote

The most fundamental aspect of learning to read is not about skills: it is about learning to behave like a reader. (Harrison, 2004, p38)

CASE STUDY 10.2

Reading poetry

This case study focuses again on children who are learning to read but who come from a background where reading is perhaps not highly valued. They are consequently reluctant readers who are finding the process of learning to read a laborious and joyless experience.

Jane is the class teacher with a Year 2 class in a primary school serving a large council estate with its attendant high crime levels and poverty. Literacy levels are of some concern throughout the school and the head teacher in consultation with the literacy coordinator has introduced a system of withdrawal for extra literacy lessons for those children struggling with their reading. The literacy coordinator has specifically requested that phonics should be the main focus for these sessions. Despite her reservations, firstly about children being identified and separated from her class in this way and secondly about the appropriateness of a diet of phonics for these particular children, Jane has no option but to accept the situation. These booster lessons in phonics take place in spare rooms or, when rooms are not available, in corridors throughout the school. Jane has noticed that the children always return from these sessions downhearted. One day Katie, one of the more vociferous members of this selected group, walks into the classroom after her phonics session and slaps her exercise book on the table protesting loudly for all to hear: *I hate reading!* Jane knows an alternative strategy must be sought if these children are ever to make progress in their reading and, perhaps more importantly, ever to find pleasure in reading. She decides that she must speak to the head teacher. This she does, eventually persuading her to suspend the phonics sessions and to allow her to try and develop the children's reading through the speaking and listening, writing and reading activities that are part of her normal classroom practice.

Jane had been sharing with the children poems from *A First Poetry Book* and the children are responding well, appearing to really enjoy listening to and talking about the poems, identifying rhyme and rhythm and words and poems that they say are their favourites. They particularly like the 'scary' poems – Eleanor Farjeon's *The Sounds in the Evening*, Jane Pridmore's *In the Dark* and James Reeves' *The Bogus-Bo*, with its humorously hideous illustration. With their appetite for poetry thoroughly whetted, Jane decides to write a class poem with the children during shared writing. This is a great success and a fun session, so much so that the children are very keen to write their own poems independently. The class is organised in mixed-ability groupings and the children have friendship pairings within these groups so these are the pairs who work together on their poems.

The children choose the subject matter – Jane suggests something from their own lives that interests them – and she supports them by talking with them about the subject they have chosen, encouraging them to extend their vocabulary to provide appropriate content for their poem. Occasionally she talks to them about rhyme and rhythm referring back to the poems they had read together in the Oxford *First Poetry Book* (Foster, 1979). Rhythm seems to be a particularly powerful stimulus for providing a hook on which to build their ideas and Jane encourages the children to compose a line, clap a rhythm and often that is all that is needed to get them started. She tells the children not to worry about rhyme too much. A successful rhyme she sees as an added bonus.

Soon Jane amasses quite a large collection of poetry written by the children. A friend of hers has a small publishing firm in her own home and she offers to publish the poems in a professional looking anthology if Jane can cover her costs by selling each one for a £1. Before publication Jane asks the children to illustrate their poems just like in the Oxford *First Poetry Book*. They now need a title for their anthology. The children decide on *Ash Tree Kids*. It is based on the name of the school but also reminds them of the 'Bash Street Kids' in their *Beano* comics. John and Robert are very influenced by the scary poems:

Mum! Mum! Look under the stairs

Something gives me the scares

It might be a dragon

It might be a snake

But it still gives me the scares

Jane would like to change the last line to *it still makes me shake* but she decides not to edit the children's poetry but to leave it as they present it to give the authentic feel of the children's own voices and also to make sure they retain ownership of their work. However, she realises that with time and appropriate questioning and discussion John and Robert would have done this editing for themselves. After a drama session about a mountain expedition Susan and Jenny wrote:

Slippy, slidey, cold

Like ice lollies, frozen

We went up the slippy slope

And went to sleep in bags

Jane ensures that every child has a poem for publication. The day the anthologies arrive there is great excitement in the classroom. Jane herself is even more excited by the impact it has on the children. Their self-esteem and confidence rise perceptibly. They become a united group of children obviously proud of their artistic abilities. This is a happy class with motivated and interested children. They begin to take pleasure in reading and appreciating each other's poems. One child tells Jane of a game they have invented around the poetry book. He would read a poem to his friends and they had to say who the writer was – gaining a point if they were correct.

Of course, the biggest impact of this poetry book is the improvement in the reading achievements of the whole class. The reading of their own words and those of their peers is clearly easier, more interesting and more meaningful than those written in many of the books they had struggled with in school. They are highly motivated to read and the children themselves seek out more poems to read to themselves and each other. JT (Jaytee), who always has a 'number 1' haircut and is one of the tougher members of the class, is a sight to behold as he marches into class flexing his muscles and chanting, *I love poetry, I love poetry!*

TO THINK ABOUT

- *Teaching should ensure that work in speaking and listening, reading and writing is integrated (National Curriculum, 2000). These three modes of English are mutually dependent and support each other.*

- **Make learning to read a real experience with real books which mirror the real lives of children.**

- **Children learn to read in different ways. Be prepared to modify your teaching if you feel children are not making progress.**

- **Share quality texts with children to inspire them to want to become good readers and writers.**

- **Show you value children's work by praise and publishing. They will then see value in their own work and in themselves as readers and writers.**

Key Quote

Frank Smith in his seminal text *Reading* (1978) advises teachers to *make learning to read easy – which means making reading a meaningful, enjoyable and frequent experience for children* (p143).

Jane had followed Frank Smith's advice (see Key Quote). She had made it meaningful by allowing the children to read their own and their friends' words drawn from their own experiences. That it was enjoyable can be seen from the reaction of the children and the excitement and enthusiasm generated in the classroom. It was frequent because learning to read had become part of the everyday experience of literacy activities in the classroom. The children were beginning to make progress in their reading but also beginning to see reading as a joyful experience.

I will conclude this chapter with a case study from my own time as a child in school. The study deals first with one negative practice which still persists in our primary schools and then with one positive practice which is not seen frequently enough.

CASE STUDY 10.3

Reading in class

Picture two classrooms. In one sits a twelve-year-old boy. The children are reading round the class. The book chosen by the teacher for this painful exercise is J. Meade Falkner's *Moonfleet*. Each child has a copy of the book – nearly three hundred pages of tiny, dense text. The child notices how long each child is asked to read and calculates which part of the text he will be asked to read. He sets to, rehearsing his selected passage in his head. The room is hot, it is a Friday afternoon. While he reads and rereads his part he is aware of one of his fellow pupils who has been chosen by the teacher to read aloud and is struggling desperately to read to the class. This particular child is one of the poorer readers in the class. The lesson is a torture for him. It will not improve his reading but perhaps, worse still, give him an antipathy to books and reading for life. Our twelve-year-old has no idea what the story is about because he is concentrating so hard on ensuring he will read well when it is his turn. Eventually, he has his turn and then the process is repeated again. He works out which will be the next part he will have to read. How many children continue to be turned off reading for life by this joyless experience? (I must point out I have since read *Moonfleet* in private in the comfort of my own home and thoroughly enjoyed it.)

The second classroom has the same child but a few years earlier. He is in a primary school classroom. It could be Friday afternoon. It would not matter because it is 3 o'clock and the children are about to be read to by their teacher. Miss Stokes has been reading E.B. White's *Charlotte's Web* to them now for over a week. She really brings the story to life reading with such expression, using different voices for the characters and always managing to finish reading at a moment of excitement in the book so that the children cannot wait until 3 o'clock the following day for the next episode. Most importantly of all she loves reading, she loves this book and her enthusiasm and love for the book is infectious. The children love it too. When they finished the book they all wrote to the author telling him how they had enjoyed it – real letters with a real audience and purpose.

In the *Times* newspaper of 20 September 2006, Jacqueline Wilson, children's author, was quoted as saying that children should be encouraged to read entire books rather than analyse only short extracts and she called for more old-fashioned reading aloud to children. She was reiterating her concerns about the National Literacy Strategy (2001) which she, along with other notable authors, including Philip Pullman, Quentin Blake, Jamila Gavin, Michael Rosen and Bernard Ashley, had highlighted in a collection of essays *Waiting for a Jamie Oliver: Beyond Bog-standard Literacy* in 2005. They expressed the view that with literacy teaching confined to a 'literacy hour' and with the demand of other subjects including a 'numeracy hour' children were being exposed to a range of extracts from books rather than whole texts. Illustrator and children's author Quentin Blake wrote, *What we object to is having our books treated as if they are frogs ready for dissection, when actually they are live frogs* (Ashley et al., 2005). These writers should be encouraged by the new Primary Framework for Literacy and Mathematics (DfES, 2006) which encourages flexibility in the teaching of literacy and the operation of the literacy hour. Ofsted (2004) reports that teachers who successfully produce avid readers regularly read novels to the class (UKLA, 2006).

TO THINK ABOUT

- Never read 'round the class' or even round the group, a practice that takes place in classrooms during what is called 'guided reading' but which is, of course, a complete misunderstanding of what guided reading was intended to be. Guided reading is about teaching children to read. If you want to refresh your understanding of the real purpose of guided reading then see NLS Framework (DfEE, 2001, p12).

- Never force a child to read aloud. Pennac (1992) describes the successful teaching of reluctant older readers in a French Lycée and he sets out the ten 'rights of readers' which he considers to be fundamental if children are to make progress in reading. These include: the right to skip pages, the right not to finish a book, the right to read anything. Harrison (2004) offers his support, describing these ten rules as 'inviolable'. Right number 1 is *the right not to read* and number 10 is *the right to remain silent*. Children cannot learn if they are anxious and for some children, even good readers, reading aloud is a stressful experience.

- Pennac's ninth 'right of the 'reader' is the right to read aloud. If children want to read aloud it may be appropriate to ask for volunteers and you may even find that some of the less competent readers will volunteer. Let them read and you will discover that children are very patient with their classmates if they know they have not been coerced into reading and are happy to try.

ACTION POINTS ACTION POINTS ACTION POINTS ACTION POINTS ACTION POINTS

> Do read aloud to children frequently.

> Set aside a time each day when you will read one of your favourite books to the children. Make it a regular part of your classroom practice.

> Remember you are the best reader in the class and you should be modelling fluent, expressive reading for the children. Read with expression and enthusiasm. Live the book and perform it.

> Never choose a book you do not like to read to children even if it is on an 'official recommended list'. Instead choose books you love. Find out about books which are good for reading aloud. Read children's books yourself and expand your own repertoire of books.

Conclusion

The puzzle of how children learn to read has still not been completely solved; that is why we talk of reading theories. Some children catch the reading 'bug' like measles; others struggle to make sense of it all. We know children learn to read in different ways and that no one theory or method will suit all children, and we know of the dangers of adopting a one-size-fits-all approach. Recent surveys show that we are getting better at teaching children to read but not getting better at teaching children that reading is enjoyable and encouraging lifelong readers. Twist et al. (2003) describe how the PIRLS (Progress in International Reading Literacy Study) in 2001 compared the reading habits and achievements of ten-year-olds in 35 countries. British children were third in the table of reading achievement but below average in terms of a positive attitude. If we are to produce lifelong readers we must be flexible in our teaching of reading and teach in a way that builds children's confidence and does not undermine it, allowing children to become valued members of our 'reading club'. Above all we must show the children in our primary classrooms that we are enthusiastic about reading, sharing our favourite books and poems with them, showing them that for us reading is a joyful experience and making them know that it can be for them, too.

Further reading

Benton, M. and Fox, G. (1987) *Teaching Literature 9–14*. Oxford: Oxford University Press.
A seminal text in the teaching of children's literature which explores how children respond to fiction and poetry and contains valuable and practical advice on how to share books and poems with children in the classroom.

Gamble, N. and Yates, S. (2002) *Exploring Children's Literature*. London: Paul Chapman Publishing.
This book will deepen your knowledge and understanding of children's literature. It will introduce you to the different genres of fiction written for children, help you to keep up to date with children's books and show you how to help children respond to books used in the classroom.

Wilson, J. (2006) *Great Books to Read Aloud*. London: Random House.
This recent publication lists and describes texts to read aloud to children aged 0–11 years recommended by publishers, booksellers, librarians and children's book experts. There is also advice on how to read the books and a clear exposition by Julia Eccleshare, children's book editor for the *Guardian* newspaper, on the benefits of reading aloud.

References

Ashley, B. et al. (2005) *Waiting for a Jamie Oliver: Beyond Bog-standard Literacy*. Reading: University of Reading.

DfEE (2001) *National Literacy Strategy Framework*. London: DfEE.

DfEE (1999) *National Curriculum*. London: DfEE.

DfES (2006) *Primary Framework for Literacy and Mathematics*. London: DfES.

Foster, J. (1979) *A First Poetry Book*. Oxford: Oxford University Press.

Harrison, C. (2004) *Understanding Reading Development*. London: Sage.

Jennings, P. (2003) *The Reading Bug ... And How to Help Your Child Catch It*. London: Penguin.

Meade Falkner, J. (1898/1993) *Moonfleet*. Oxford: Oxford Paperbacks.

Pennac, D. (1992) *Reads Like a Novel*, trans. Daniel Dunn. London: Quartet Books.

Riley, J. (1999) *Teaching Reading at Key Stage One and Before*. Cheltenham: Stanley Thornes.

Smith, F. (1978) *Reading*. Cambridge: Cambridge University Press.

Twist, L., Sainsbury, M., Woodthorpe, A. and Whetton, C. (2003) *Reading All Over the World: The PIRLS National Report for England*. Slough: NFER.

UKLA (2006) *Submission to the Review of Best Practice in the Teaching of Early Reading*. Royston: UKLA.

White, E.B. (1952,1969) *Charlotte's Web*. London: Penguin/Puffin.

11
The joy of learning poetry off by heart
Linda Pagett

Introduction

You may already be switched on to poetry. You may have shelves groaning with anthologies and the works of favourite poets. You may have a classroom where children bring poems to share, are eager to perform and look to you as a doyen(ne) of poetic works, someone who enthuses them, guides them, can always find just the right poem for the right occasion and perhaps most of all reads aloud to them regularly. But I doubt it! A recent poll of postgraduate students I teach revealed that most are 'scared' of poetry. Scared? Scared of what? Scared of poems like *Pat a Cake Pat a Cake Baker's Man*, which children still chant and clap in playgrounds? Scared of *I Must Go Down to the Sea Again*, which makes anyone sitting typing, as I am now, feel desperately suburban. Scared of Ted Hughes' poem *My Brother Bert*, famous for having a mouse in his shirt? Some poems *are* scary of course. Emily Brontë begins her lyric poem *Song* with these lines:

The night is darkening round me
The wild winds coldly blow

But no! These students are scared of *teaching* poetry because they think they cannot do it. They think they cannot do it because they are also frightened of *learning* poetry. They think it is too hard. If you are a scaredy cat too, then this is just the chapter for you. In reading on you may become convinced that poetry can run through the fabric of the school day. It can be an art form that blends in with others to support drama, performance, art and design and most of all children's thinking so that they take language seriously and begin to aspire to finding the right words in the right order – other people's and their own.

Background

Humans don't seem to be able to manage without poetry. It is all around us in various forms including songs, plays and advertising jingles, and seems to be an integral part of society. Poetry for children in the eighteenth century was intended to teach children *good manners, conventional behaviour and religious observance* (Styles, 1998, p1). It was intended to help save the souls of children, all of whom were thought to be born into original sin and needed to be rescued from the devil. Romanticism softened this a little in the nineteenth century and gave us many classic nursery rhymes such as *Twinkle Twinkle Little Star*. Sentimental verses, often very obviously written for children, provided a contrasting backdrop to the new wave poets of the 1960s. This was a time of huge social change. Regionalism took off, encouraging people to value their home languages and dialect and this encouraged the Liverpool school of poets, people like Roger McGough and Brian Patten who wrote funny, streetwise work that resonated with a wider circle of children than more formal verse, written for the 'nannied' classes. Since the 1960s Britain has become more multicultural and this has supported the development of poetry in 'other Englishes'. Poets such as Benjamin Zephania, Grace Nichols and John Agard have inspired children to think beyond standard formal English in their reading and writing.

Education in primary schools before the introduction of a National Curriculum in 1989 was a largely ad hoc affair. Teachers had free reign in organising the curriculum, apart from religious observance. This meant that if your teacher was very keen on poetry you probably did quite a lot of it. If you were lucky enough to have a teacher who was keen on music and poetry you would have sung along to various poetic forms: hymns, songs, rounds, etc. However, if your teacher was wary of poetry or simply did not like it you may not have experienced much of it at all.

The National Curriculum (NC) takes poetry very seriously. Teachers are advised that children in both Key Stages 1 and 2 should hear poetry read aloud, retell, reread or dramatise familiar stories and poems, and have plenty of opportunity to write poetry. The NC requires children to learn, recite and act out stories and poems, identify patterns of rhythm, rhyme and sounds, and respond imaginatively in different ways to what they read. Older children have to consider poetic forms and their effects and recognise the choice, use and effect of figurative language, vocabulary and patterns of language. Thus poetry has become firmly embedded in the curriculum. The National Literacy Strategy (NLS) builds upon the NC and stipulates that various forms of poetry be taught including: classic, modern poetry, prayers, epitaphs, thin poems, shape poems and many more. The NLS gives teachers specific guidance in their teaching and emphasises the importance of reading aloud, performance and using existing poems as models for writing. It *lays consistent stress on the interplay between listening to, reading, writing and performing poetry* (Beard, 1999, p46). Children are required to read and write poetry every term.

TO THINK ABOUT
TO THINK ABOUT

- Even young children are fascinated by rhyme, language play, puns, silly jokes and jingles which help to teach how language works.

- Children who can understand and manipulate rhyme learn to read more easily (Goswami, 1999).

- Poetry needs to be read aloud as techniques such as alliteration are spoken, not written. The words 'naughty gnat' only have the same beginning when you say them.

- Not all poems have rhyme or verse or even use figurative language such as similes and metaphors.

- Poetry doesn't have to be written down. This was impossible in pre-literate society; nevertheless people passed down poems and stories which they had rote learned. Playground poems emerge in spoken form such as:

Ooh! Ah! I've lost me bra

I've left me knickers in me boyfriend's car

(Styles, 1998, xxvi)

The impact of joyful poetry on children

Children are arriving at school. Angela is wearing a green wig. She spots me from across the playground, runs up, dons a huge pair of spectacles she's painstakingly decorated with feathers and says, *Miss Pagett, wad'ya think?* I'm cautious. I can see her mother out of the corner of my eye.

Very nice.

But will it do?

What for?

She then reels off the poem, *My Sister Jane* by Ted Hughes, which describes a bird which is trying to look human by wearing a wig:

> *And dark spectacles – a huge pair*
> *To cover her very crowy stare*

A little crowd has gathered, including Alex who has got a trident and a red devil mask. Angela's mother comes up to tell me how pleased she is that Angela has a part in the poetry show. Apparently she knows all her poems and everyone else's. We then go into school and the children rehearse. They find their own space in the room and ask friends to help. They make suggestions like, *Why don't you fall over when you get to the line: 'She'll knock you dead'*?

I work with one group of three children, who are using musical instruments: a shaker, a tambourine and a Chinese wood block. They have choices with their short poem. It can be recited in various ways including the use of multiple voices. They decide to do it as a 'round', consisting of three recitations each, and start and finish with perfect timing. Natalie and Joan are practising a poem from *Please Mrs Butler* (Ahlberg, 1990). They have a mock fight, where they pretend to pull each other's hair and wrestle but it is controlled. Darren is practising a Benjamin Zephania poem. It is not easy but he has listened to Benjamin on video and has captured the patois well. Julie and Samantha are giggling over their poem *My Iguana*. It has a wonderful rolling rhythm and cadence that they pick up drumming their nails on tambourines in accompaniment. They have watched the poet himself, Brian Moses, perform this on the *Poetry Archive* website and feel inspired by the way in which he uses musical instruments to accompany his work. Trevor has special educational needs but he loves poetry performance. Although he finds reading and writing poetry independently difficult, he has learnt a chain poem the class have made up together, which extends a traditional rhyme:

> *'Fire! Fire!' said Mrs Dyer*
> *'Where, where?' said Mrs Dare*
> *'Over there,' said Mrs Bear*
> *'Get some water,' said Mrs Slaughter*

He decides to perform alternate verses with Barry, who joined the school two weeks ago. Barry was reluctant to join in any performance work to begin with so he acted as a critical friend helping others but now he is ready to join in. All the children are completely absorbed and confident in what they are doing. Because they have learnt the words their bodies are free to concentrate on performance. They have a variety of techniques to choose from: freeze frame, tableaux, multiple voices, using musical instruments, mime and the opportunity to work alone or with others.

My role is one of orchestration, simply suggesting an order and making sure we all arrive at the venue with some time for the children to get used to their new space. My role is not as important now as I have established a strong poetry culture in the school, so that children are introduced to poetry by enthusiastic teachers. It is read to the children regularly in slots of a few moments, for example in getting them settled for registration.

A simple way of getting children's attention is simply to start one of the poems you know off by heart as a class. They automatically join in. Poetry posters around the school offer frequent opportunities for children to read, write and perform. Within this culture there is the chance to do some focused poetry work, which explores meaning beyond the literal, but even here the thinking time is prefaced with teacher reading aloud so that children develop the inner tunes of an experienced poet. 'Inner tunes' are a repertoire of phrases and patterned language such as rhyme, which we can internalise and call upon in writing our own poetry. They help us hear a poem in our heads even as we read silently.

ACTION POINTS ACTION POINTS ACTION POINTS ACTION POINTS ACTION POINTS

> Demonstration is important but will not happen unless the children need to have opportunities to hear poetry read well, with intelligence and enthusiasm. This includes listening to teachers but also using websites, video material and wherever possible the chance to see live performance.

> If children are to choose poems and build their own repertoire they need access to a choice of quality books.

> Speaking and listening are important parts of poetry writing. Children need to develop an 'inner ear' when reading poetry that enables them to map the rhythm onto the words as they read.

> Children find learning off by heart easy. Don't underestimate how much they can learn.

> Parents can be involved. Inviting them to performances or readings is one way of emphasising the importance of poetry in the curriculum.

Innovative and creative approaches in teaching poetry

In your desire to promote innovative and creative approaches, take note of the following.

Poetry can be powerful

Poetry can be powerful – not if it is locked in the pages of an unopened book but if it is read and engaged with. It can enable us to look afresh at fairly mundane things, affect our emotions and make us think. Many texts can do this, but poetry is more memorable and so we have it to hand more easily. It is often figurative and so creates pictures in the mind; the rhythms stay with us and resonate around our heads, so poetry is a form where both visual and aural aspects explore the way that meaning is created. Ted Hughes thought of poems as a kind of animal creation:

> They have their own life, like animals, by which I mean that they seem quite sepa-rate from any person, even from their author, and nothing can be added to them or taken away without maiming and perhaps even killing them. And they have a cer-tain wisdom. They know something special ... (Hughes, 1967, p15)

If you accept that poetry is important it can make you even more nervous in your teach-ing but this fear is completely unfounded. Children are natural performers; they are still fascinated by language and poems are often short enough to capture even timid readers and writers.

Poetry is inclusive

Pupils can cope with quite challenging ideas because poems do not require the reading stamina of longer texts. Children can hold the whole text in their thinking as they try to make sense of it. Even longer poems are often easier to read than other texts. This is because rolling rhythm and metre, rhyming patterns and choruses help us to anticipate what is coming next. Struggling readers can often become quite fluent when reading poetry. Robert was a struggling reader but he loved *The Lady of Shallott* by Alfred Lord Tennyson, a long, romantic poem which he practised reading and eventually wrote his own poem which refers to the mirror into which the Lady looked each day as she was forbidden by a witch's curse to look through the windows.

> *Shadows darken my daytime,*
> *Daytime is not long for me,*
> *My life is nothing,*
> *Nothing but shadows*

(Robert, aged 8)

This is evidence of deep involvement in a poem which he struggled to read independently. Julie liked the poem too. Her home life had a particular savagery about it but she could escape into this fairy tale and she readily took the part of the lady, dressed in snowy white. Literature gives us what Benton and Fox have called a 'secondary world' to escape into (1985, p2). It is an amalgam of our and the author's imaginations through the medium of the text.

Poetry can underpin language development generally

Halliday (1975) proposed three important ideas.

- **We learn language.**
- **We learn about language.**
- **We learn through language.**

Poetry enables us to learn language

Our very first encounters with literature may be lullabies and nursery rhymes. We hear and chant them long before we have an understanding of the inherent ideas. Poetry enables us to learn what is often described as book language – poetic or literary language, such as:

> *Jack be nimble*
> *Jack be quick*
> *Jack jump over the candlestick*

(Anon.)

Candlestick and nimble are unusual words for children in the early years but they can learn this rhyme easily. When reciting, you can actually feel Jack running up to the stick in the first two lines, taking a deep breath and then jumping safely over in the third. It is fun and memorable.

Poetry enables us to learn about language

We understand that poems can be long or short, fat or thin, rhyming or not; that punctuation is very different from the way it is used in prose. Sometimes it is at the end of every line: sometimes a full stop signals the end of a poem, sometimes not. We are more likely to encounter colons and semi colons. We identify rhyming patterns, which can support phonological awareness, an understanding of the sound system of a language and, later, spelling (Goswami, 1999). In the nursery rhyme *Jack and Jill*, for example, we hear the rhyme Jill and hill. When we see it written down we can see the spelling pattern which helps us in tackling other words such as pill, still, etc. Other language features we come to know through poetry include alliteration, as in the tongue twister:

She sells sea shells on the sea shore
The shells she sells are sea shells I'm sure

And assonance as in the line: *I do not like you bully night* from a poem by Roger McGough. Similes and metaphors can create images in our mind. Ted Hughes, for example, in his poem *The Snail* writes:

With skin all wrinkled
Like a whale
On a ribbon of sea
Comes the moonlit snail

(Hughes, in Morpurgo, 2001, p83)

There is a challenging simile here about a whale, one of the earth's biggest creatures, and a snail, one of the smallest, and a metaphor which compares the snail's slime to the sea. Hughes then goes on in the poem to describe the snail as 'God's tongue' and 'God's kiss', arresting images which may come back to us every time we see a snail and its grey muscley foot.

Poetry can help us learn through language

We need to talk about poetry in order to understand why we like or dislike it or what it means. It may not of course mean the same thing to all readers. This is a transcript of pupils talking about Hughes' poem *My Other Granny*, in which he describes his family of sea creatures. Three children discuss the lines:

When the world rolls blind
As a boulder in the night-sea surf

Here are a few of their comments:

Child A: *It makes you feel it's (the world) not seeing and it's just going anywhere.*

Child B: *It makes me think like the sea is all big and the world is turned all small.*

Child C: *Say it's (the world) rolling down the hill. It wouldn't care if a car was in front of it – it would just smack into it.*

The children are visualising a world made reckless, frustrated and powerless in the face of the great energy of the oceans. They are thinking at quite a deep level about the writer's motives and each child has the opportunity to listen to others. Together they are using language to learn: to interpret and picture what Hughes intended the reader to under-stand. Drawing pictures can support this process. In Figure 11.1 we see how a child has visualised the power of a storm so intense the world is rolling blindly, pushed along by the waves; sea creatures are thrown up into the air with tentacles and claws flailing.

Figure 11.1 Child's visualisation of a storm

Strategies in teaching poetry

You may be convinced that poetry is important and can be a joy to teach but your question might still be, 'How do I do it?' Here are some useful starting points.

Build on the known

Find out what the children already know and celebrate it. Persuade pupils to share favourite playground chants and claps, pop songs – in fact, anything they already enjoy.

Get a good quantity of poems – screen and book based

Try to make the choice eclectic to involve more children. Everyone likes humorous verse so this is often good for starters but children need to build a repertoire of different types of poetry and you can introduce them to forms which are more challenging than those they might find independently, for instance ballads or haiku.

Read aloud to children

Encourage them to learn off by heart. You can scaffold this quite easily by, for example, reading a poem with a chorus to the children. I am thinking here of something like the *Jumblies* by Edward Lear. Encourage the children to join in the chorus;

> *Their hands are blue and their heads are green*
> *And they went to sea in a sieve*

And then hand over individual verses to certain children. Having a performance line on the floor is a good idea with infants. They stand next to each other on the line and each recites one line of a simple poem such as:

> *There she goes*
> *There she goes*
> *All dressed up in her Sunday clothes*

> (Anon.)

Standing in line helps them stay focused on the pace and delivery of the poem and when they have memorised it you can experiment by using multiple voices: one voice for line one, two voices for line two and three voices for line three. When the children have mastered this add movement. The children delivering the first two lines can point enthusiastically and the third child can put on a pretty hat and walk grandly around the others. In this way you have built up the poem in a sequence listen → recite → perform. The same teaching sequence can be used for much longer poems.

Encourage children to pay focused attention to meaning

A good context for this is performance; you cannot perform if you do not understand the work but sometimes you will choose only to read and discuss poetry. Annotating your poem, perhaps on the interactive whiteboard, can help you remember important teaching points, e.g. how should this be read, slowly or quickly? where does the pace quicken? what does the poet mean by this phrase? what pictures come into your mind here?

Scaffold discussion

Benton and Fox (1985) make various suggestions such as giving children poems with some words blocked out which they have to guess, cutting up poems in lines to be rearranged in the 'best' order and even inserting some wrong words to see if children can spot them. In this way children come to know what poetry is and are ready to write their own.Try stimulating children in various ways to write. If, for example, you want the children to write about a river, take them to see one. Rebecca wrote this poem after seeing a river with its trout rings, salmon leaps and otter haunts:

Oh how I love the river!
Oh how I love its moods and the wonderful trout rings and the salmon leaping,
Oh how I'd love to go swimming with an otter,
A lovely, brown furry otter
In that cold rushing river
On a hot steamy day

(Rebecca, aged 8)

Rebecca has a real feeling here for the cool movement of the river that is difficult to manufacture in what might be a hot, stuffy classroom.

Use existing models of poems to write in the same style

A simple example of this is the traditional poem:

One potato
Two potatoes
Three potatoes four
Five potatoes
Six potatoes
Seven potatoes
More!

(Anon.)

That can quickly become:

One banana, two bananas ... or One tomato, two tomatoes ...

In this way the words have changed but the syllables remain the same, giving us the original structure and rhyme but an understanding of how syllabic patterns work.

Use musical instruments to help children respond to rhythm and metre

For example, in the *One potato poem* above, a sharp smack on the Chinese woodblock for the numbers followed by a shake of the tambourine for potatoes can lift a performance.

Write around a poem to deepen a child's response

Here is an example of a child writing to the Lady of Shalott.

> *Dear Lady of Shalott*
> *I have heard your singing many times before. O, can't you come down? I have*
> *longed to see you. Oh please come down and tell me all about yourself. Do you*
> *know why I know you, because I often hear you singing when I go by on my*
> *ambling pad.*
>
> From Frederick, Abbot of Camelot

This pupil has taken the words 'ambling pad' directly from the poem – evidence that his command of language is enriched by the poem.

Support children's engagement through drama and art

For example, Hughes' poem *My Other Granny* could be the basis of a drama lesson where children are pretending to be sea creatures on a wild, wet, windy night. They could practise movements: sidling, slithering, spilling out of the surf to the accompaniment of some appropriate music. Paired work between the octopus and the grandchild can be the basis for 'a conversation', where the grandchild tries to persuade Granny to talk. There are various solutions to this problem: perhaps Granny is happy to write or speak with an interpreter or perhaps there is someone else, a witch perhaps, who can help her talk. Children then explain to others why they think Granny was reluctant to talk, how they helped her and what she said. The poem could stimulate art work; for example, a corner of the classroom could become a seascape with collages of fish, models of sea creatures, textiles which represent waves, seaweed and spray. Children can become closer to a poem if they integrate it into work across the curriculum.

Employ ICT to record work

Children's poems can be printed on top of images which can include scanned drawings, digital photographs or images found on the internet. Children's own drawings can be scanned into a computerised slide presentation and then the voices recorded as children recite their work. Figure 11.2 shows an example of children reciting the *Pied Piper of Hamlyn* by Robert Browning on top of their own illustrations.

Figure 11.2 Child's use of ICT and poetry

Videoing performance can help children criticise their work and commend good practice.

ACTION POINTS ACTION POINTS ACTION POINTS ACTION POINTS ACTION POINTS

> Get together with other schools to organise a poetry swapshop where you visit each other to offer performances and readings.

> Always have a poem 'on the go' in the class. Pin up the first verse one day, the next verse the next, etc. so that children are desperate to read what comes next.

> Let children have photocopies of poems to annotate for themselves so that they decide how they are going to read aloud, for example 'quietly lines 1 and 2; loudly lines 4 and 5'.

> Encourage children to talk about golden lines in poetry, saying which is their 'golden line', i.e. the one they like best.

> Let children draft and redraft their poetry. Leave it alone for a while to mature and then let it catch you by surprise. Poems can have lives of their own.

Conclusion

I hope that I have managed to convince you that it can be a joy to teach poetry. Children grow in confidence as they master the reading and writing of sophisticated forms of language and the language stays with them. We read and write various text types in school: reports, explanations, instructions, and these are important. We gain knowledge and understanding of the world from them but the language does not stay with us in the same way. Children with a rich diet of poetic experience have to hand their own compendium of lyric language to express themselves in speech and writing. They will never be scared of poetry because they know it belongs to them.

Further reading

King, J. and Pagett, L. (2006) Poetry gallery. *The Primary English Magazine*, 11 (5), 18–22.
King and Pagett explain how to use ICT to present poetry.

Pagett, L. and Somers, J. (2004) *Off by Heart: Performing and Presenting Poetry in the Primary School*. Sheffield: National Association of Teachers of English.
This text is especially suitable for teachers who are wary of poetry as it very simply describes how to inspire children to perform. There are simple lesson plans for Key Stages 1 and 2 and suggestions for how to use ICT to make screen-based texts.

References

Ahlberg, A. (1990) *Please Mrs. Butler*. London: Kestrel Books.

Beard, R. (1998) *National Literacy Strategy Review of Research and Other Related Evidence*. Sudbury: DfEE Publication.

Benton, M. and Fox, G. (1985) *Teaching Literature, Nine to Fourteen*. Oxford: Oxford University Press.

DfES (1998) *The National Literacy Strategy Framework for Teaching*. London: DfES.

DfES/QCA (2000) *The National Curriculum Handbook for Teachers*. London: DfES.

Goswami, U. (1999) Causal connections in beginning reading: the importance of rhyme. *Journal of Research in Reading*, 22 (3), 217–40.

Halliday, M.A.K. (1975) *Language as a Social Semiotic: The Social Interpretation of Language and Meaning*. London: Edward Arnold.

Hughes, T. (1967) *Poetry in the Making*. London: Faber and Faber.

Hughes, T. (2001) The snail, in M. Morpurgo (ed.) *Because a Fire Was in My Head*. London: Faber.

Styles, M. (1998) *From the Garden to the Street: Three Hundred Years of Poetry for Children*. London: Cassell.

12
The joy of mathematics
Nick Pratt and John Berry

Introduction

There are few subjects that polarise people like mathematics. Individuals tend to express a strong love or intense dislike of the subject; for adults, all too often the latter. This generally negative view has strange consequences, namely that people often seem almost proud to be 'no good at maths' in a way that would be unheard of in other subjects. More seriously it has negative effects for our society as a whole because of falling numbers of mathematics graduates and a wider population that seems to find using mathematics for everyday reasoning difficult. (If you don't believe us read John Allen Paulos' book, *Innumeracy*, 2000.)

So, is there a secret to creating a positive approach to the subject? What particular form of 'joyfulness' could it encourage? This chapter offers the authors' ideas about what seems to matter in terms of helping learners, young *or* old, to discover joy in mathematics. Maths can be en*joy*able ... if you understand what it's about.

> **TO THINK ABOUT**
>
> Can you write a dictionary definition of both 'art' and 'mathematics'? Try it now yourself. What would a dictionary say about each one?

We cannot know what you wrote in trying the 'To think about' task but we can tell you that for the majority of people the first definition is easier to write than the second. Art seems clear. Even not being experts in the subject, we have a strong sense of a *process*, the process of creating images/objects perhaps, making use of artistic techniques in order to represent the world in some new way. In other words art provides a way of making sense of the world. Note too that so does history ... and geography ... and science. All these subjects are readily seen as a means of understanding our surroundings. When people talk about maths though, they tend to focus more on the 'content' (usually of the school curriculum). They describe the techniques and tools, adding, subtracting, etc. but do not see this in terms of a process. In other words, maths is not something you *do*, it is something you *know*.

As an adult you will have enjoyed/been subjected to/endured (delete as applicable) over 2,000 hours of maths teaching – roughly 11 years, 200 days a year for an hour a day. That is a long time not to 'do' anything and, we believe, lies at the heart of why so many adults report a lack of (en)*joy*(ment) in the subject.

> **ACTION POINT** ACTION POINT ACTION POINT ACTION POINT ACTION POINT
>
> > Try asking the children in your class what mathematics means to them. What do their answers imply for your teaching?

What does 'doing' mathematics look like?

Although learners may get enjoyment from knowing a lot of mathematical information, what we are suggesting here is that maths must be a subject which involves *doing* something. Again, there is room for confusion. We do not mean 'getting things done' (completing worksheets or exercises – though we might still do this sometimes); we mean *acting mathematically* towards things. To do this demands knowing what it means to *act mathematically*.

Rather than give a list here, we offer you a case study which we hope provides a mathematical picture. Having read it we will be in a better position to unpick the features of mathematical work. At this stage though we want to introduce three key themes that we will return to in detail and which, together, will form the basis for finding joy in mathematical work. These are:

- **weaving together the 'mathematical' and 'physical' worlds;**
- **understanding mathematical work *geometrically* (i.e. through pictures) and *graphically* (i.e. through diagrams), not just numerically;**
- **making use of key mathematical processes – knowing what it means to 'do' mathematics.**

Finally, you will notice that the case study is not a lesson but a mathematical event over a whole day. We have done this deliberately to challenge some ideas about the way maths is structured in schools. For now though, bear with us; we will be aiming to suggest how this can be reorganised so that it forms part of classroom practice.

CASE STUDY 12.1

Fibonacci numbers

Joe (10) and Chris (11) are involved in a day-long mathematics event exploring the 'Fibonacci sequence' and how it relates to the world around them. The day begins with an activity on sequences which Joe and Chris work on for approximately 15 minutes. A learning objective is shared with the children, but in the form of a question: 'What can we find out about *sequences* and how they work?'

ACTIVITY: Find the next number

For each of the following sequences, write down the next two terms [you might like to do this yourself before reading on]:

A.	5,	8,	13,	20,			
B.	21,	15,	9,	3,			
C.	10,	8,	4,	–2,			
D.	1,	8,	27,	64,	125,		
E.	0,	1,	1,	2,	3,	5,	8,

Joe and Chris work out sequences A, B and C easily, as in each case the 'first differences' (i.e. the difference between consecutive numbers at the first level) are a simple pattern. Having written the next two terms for each one, the teacher encourages them to *generalise* the sequence and to explain in words 'how it works'. By deliberately pretending to disagree with them, she forces the boys to *justify* their reasoning in order to convince her, and they have great fun arguing their case and sticking up for their mathematical ideas (against the 'authority' of the teacher).

Sequence D provides the first stumbling block for the day. Various 'theories' emerge from the class, but when the teacher asks the children 'to convince us', their mathematics is quickly seen to be inaccurate and the theories fall down. Joe and Chris are well trained in looking at first differences but have not gone further to look at second and third differences (i.e. differences between differences, etc.). Sequence D initiates a teacher-led discussion with all pupils coming to see that the third differences are 6. One pair of pupils identifies the sequence as the cube numbers (i.e. 1^3, 2^3, 3^3, etc.). The children then explore *square* numbers and note that the second differences are equal (to 2) this time. From this, the class forms a *conjecture*: that a sequence of numbers with power 'n' will have constant differences at the nth level. Like the other pupils, Joe and Chris need to be led through this idea, but are happy to make the conjecture and then spend a few minutes testing it with powers of four and five (and the use of an interactive calculator on the whiteboard).

Sequence E again poses a challenge. Each term is the *sum* of the two preceding terms – the Fibonacci sequence and the theme for the day's work. Joe has seen this sequence before and the whisper of knowledge starts to spread round the room. The teacher spends a little time talking about the life of Leonardo Fibonacci, who was born in Italy and lived between 1180 and 1250, and recounts something of his early ideas about this sequence. Joe and Chris, along with most of the pupils, seem interested in this 'human' side to mathematics.

The teacher picks up on the Fibonacci sequence and Joe and Chris have fun briefly identifying how the numbers fit their body. One nose, one mouth, two eyes, two ears, two hands, two thumbs, eight fingers and so on. This leads to the idea of where the Fibonacci numbers appear in the world around us. The teacher leads the discussion towards the occurrence of Fibonacci numbers in plants. The photographs in Figure 12.1 are displayed on the interactive whiteboard and the pupils are asked to look carefully at them.

pink

poppy seed head

lily

Figure 12.1 Photographs of flowers

They notice that there are five petals on the pinks and 13 ridges on the poppy seed head – Fibonacci numbers. For the lily the pupils count six petals, but in fact three of these are *sepals*, which form the outer protection of the flower when in bud. The other three are petals … again, Fibonacci numbers. The teacher has photos of other flowers for the children to explore, as follows:

3 petals: lily, iris

5 petals: buttercup, wild rose, pinks

8 petals: delphiniums

13 petals: some daisies, ragwort

21 petals: aster, chicory

A passion flower takes some examining but eventually reveals three sepals and five outer green petals followed by an inner layer of five more paler green petals. A front view shows 144 thin blue petals – another Fibonacci number.

The pupils are fascinated that Fibonacci numbers occur in this way in nature and this leads to a homework task exploring flowers at home. After this excursion into the physical world, the children return to the sequence itself and explore what happens when fractions are formed from Fibonacci numbers. The teacher encourages them to 'play with numbers' and look for patterns.

A new sequence is made by creating fractions using consecutive pairs of Fibonacci numbers (larger divided by the smaller). For example, the first four new terms are **1** (1/1), **2** (2/1), **1.5** (3/2) and **1.6666667** (5/3). Using calculators, the children work on this new sequence, as follows:

1, 2, 1.5, 1.6666667, 1.6, 1.625, 1.6153846, 1.619048, 1.617647, 1.618182, 1.617978, 1.6180556, 1.6180258, 1.6180371, 1.6180327, 1.6180344, 1.6180338, 1.6180341, 1.6180339, 1.6180339, 1.6180339

Joe and Chris draw a graph of the results and notice how the sequence of fractions creates a wavy line which then settles down to the particular number 1.6180339 – a *converging sequence*. According to Joe's calculator the sequence appears to become 1.6180339 but Chris's calculator gives 1.6180340. They are surprised at the difference and this provides an opportunity to talk about how calculators might round off numbers that appear to go on forever.

This number is called the *golden ratio* or the *golden number*, for which mathematicians have chosen a special symbol: the Greek letter Phi or Φ. Having found the pattern, the children explore how this golden number appears in many situations, e.g. in art, in the human body, in architecture. One example used is the Parthenon in Athens, now in ruins, whose dimensions were all based on this golden number. Using photographs and drawings, the children explore this relationship.

Before leaving the ratios, Chris asks what would happen if the fractions were turned upside down, i.e. the smaller over the larger in the consecutive pairs. The pupils enthusiastically set to work and are fascinated to discover that the sequence of fractions converges to 0.6180339 – in other words, the golden number minus 1. This number is denoted by phi ϕ (similar to Phi but with a small p). The teacher herself models some 'playing' with numbers on the whiteboard and shows that: Phi – phi = 1 and Phi × phi = 1.

The final part of the day is to represent the Fibonacci sequence in a diagram. Using squared paper, the children draw 'Fibonacci squares' (squares with sides of length equal to a Fibonacci number). Working outwards from the middle, the smallest square has side length 1, leading to a square of length 2, then one of length 3, and so on. They then impose a Fibonacci spiral, formed by drawing quarter circles in each square, as shown in Figure 12.2.

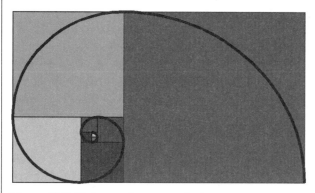
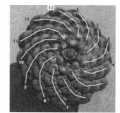

Figure 12.2 Pictures of curve and pine cone

The day concludes with more examples of the occurrence of Fibonacci spirals in nature, from the internal chambers of a Nautilus sea shell to the 13 spirals on a pine cone. At the end, Chris and Joe are asked to comment on their day. As Joe says:

The Fibonacci sequence was amazing as you could make the golden ratio from it. Seeing Fibonacci in everything was great and very interesting.

Key features of mathematical work

Case study 12.1 has offered an illustration of what mathematical work might look like. What, though, were the key features of it? What made it mathematical *and* enjoyable?

ACTION POINTS ACTION POINTS ACTION POINTS ACTION POINTS ACTION POINTS

Go back through the case study, considering:

> **how the mathematical context and the 'physical world' context interrelated;**

> **how work with numbers was integrated with pictures and diagrams;**

> **whether or not you could identify processes that you see as fundamental to mathematical work;**

> **how the example relates to *your* classroom context and to younger, and/or less able, children.**

We wonder what you made of the questions in the Action Points? Since we cannot know, we share with you our perspective, not because we think it is 'true' but because we hope it has something to offer you in (re)thinking about mathematics.

First, it is noticeable that the example does not start with a problem to solve. Instead, it presents children with a mathematical idea to consider (sequences) and, importantly, presents this in a problematic (or puzzling) way – that is to say, a way that encourages the pupils to *investigate* something in pursuit of a solution. We think this is a really important point. Joy in mathematics is often associated with the feeling of having resolved a puzzle or seen a new insight/connection in some way. If children only ever see problems as one-off events, done on an occasional basis (often Fridays), it implies that there is a whole side to maths that is *not* about problems. This quickly becomes simply 'stuff' to be learnt, which is never very exciting. We advocate *all* mathematics being set in a problematic context, whether it is a relatively sophisticated idea such as the Fibonacci sequence above, or five-year-olds learning the counting numbers by being asked to 'spot the missing number' from the sequence 1, 2, 3, 5, 6, 7, 8, 9, 10.

If you want to understand this point from a more theoretical perspective, what we are saying is that the way the curriculum is organised, with its content and problem-solving strands separated from each other, tends to suggest an 'acquire and apply' model of learning. Skills and knowledge are first acquired and then made use of. From this perspective, children cannot do any problem-solving until some knowledge has been 'delivered' to them. Our view is different. *What* children know is situated in the *way* they learn it; by continuously resolving problematic situations which involve the ideas, skills and knowledge from the curriculum, they actually learn something *different* from that which they would by learning it 'out of context' to then 'apply' (see Boaler, 2002).

By way of example, think about gardening. Do you become a gardener by first learning it from a book and then just going to do it? Well you can do, but what you learn would be different from simply getting on with some gardening and solving garden problems (how do I plan this border?). Of course you may still use books and TV programmes to help you learn to garden, just as teachers will still directly teach children ideas to use in their problem-solving. But the learning needs to be rooted (literally for gardeners) in the fundamental business of the practice – gardening for the green fingered, and in the same way, using mathematics to solve puzzles and problems for the mathematician.

A second point about the way the case study dealt with problems is that not only were all situations presented 'problematically' but the context for this alternated between the mathematical world (working on the sequences), the physical world (seeing how the ideas related to flowers) and back into the mathematical again (a new sequence and the *golden ratio*). All too often, school maths operates only in one direction – how the mathematical world can be used 'in practice' in the real world. Children should not just be learning maths in order to 'use' it (again this implies that acquire–apply model) but should be seeing the opportunity to develop new mathematical ideas from physical (or indeed other mathematical) contexts. Learning maths and doing maths are not separate in this model. They come as one.

Has this got anything to do with joyfulness in maths? Well yes, we think it is central because children, like Joe in the case study, tend not to say, 'Thanks miss/sir, that will be *useful*', but they do often say, 'Thanks miss/sir, that is *interesting*'. Do you see our point? Young children do not usually care very much whether something is useful in everyday life. They want things to be fascinating, which solving puzzles and seeing connections is. This is what maths should be for them.

Just as importantly, if problematic situations and puzzles are the way we learn maths, this then opens it up to the younger and the less able, since we have moved away from the idea that you have to know lots first before being let loose on problems. For example, rather than just learning all the number bonds to ten as numerical facts, being given ten teddy bears and finding all the ways to make two groups with them (perhaps in relation to a discussion about friendship groups) is much more interesting. Drawing this, and then relating it to the numerical version, can follow in due course.

ACTION POINTS ACTION POINTS ACTION POINTS ACTION POINTS ACTION POINTS

> Think about the lesson objectives you use in your maths teaching. If they are statements, (You will learn that ...) turn them into questions so that every lesson is centred around something puzzling to solve: What happens when ...? How can we ...? What is the most efficient way to...?

> See the publication from Devon Curriculum Services (2005) in the Further Reading below for ideas here.

Integrating number work with geometry and diagrams

Ask children to give an example of some mathematics they have done at school and the chances are they will tell you something about numbers. Numerical work dominates the curriculum. This is a real mistake. It helps learners if they see and touch things, as well as write and talk about them. It is fortunate, then, that there are two whole branches of mathematics that are about shape and space and about representing things graphically and these need to be connected to number, not seen as separate from it. Geometrical images, numerical symbols and graphical/pictorial representations can often be used to illustrate and understand *the same* mathematical idea, as in the case study where the golden ratio was understood in terms of numbers, a graph and geometrically through a diagram of squares. This approach makes things more inclusive too, since children who find numbers difficult will have other, more accessible, ways to understand ideas.

Making use of key mathematical processes

It is not uncommon for us in our work with young and trainee teachers to hear someone proudly claiming that they had planned a lesson in such a way that the children did not even know it was maths. There can be two meanings implied here: first that children were making use of their maths in such a seamless way that they did not need to recognise it as such (perhaps Joe and Chris were like this); second that children dislike it so much that it needs to be hidden away – like medicine, mixed in with some sweet drink so as not to be noticed. While we hope that the nonsensicalness of the second of these is obvious, the first needs unpicking a little. Clearly, cross-curricular work, where children view a situation from a range of perspectives and see it in a more holistic way, is a good thing. On the other hand, mathematics, like all subjects, offers very particular ways in which a situation can be understood. Indeed, Ian Stewart suggests that a good definition of a mathematician is someone *who sees opportunities for doing mathematics that the rest of us miss* (Stewart, 1997, p1). Mathematics offers people powerful opportunities because of the *particular* way of acting and thinking that it involves. Here, we consider just three aspects of such mathematical thinking.

- **Conjecture – the practice of considering *what might happen* (and why).**
- **Generalisation – the practice of seeing *patterns and rules* from particular examples.**
- **Proof – the practice of being able to justify clearly and logically *why* something is as it is.**

All too often these processes are thought of as for older learners of mathematics, but this need not be the case. At the primary level they can be enacted through a set of simple questions, as follows …

To encourage children to *conjecture*, ask questions.

- **Can you guess what will happen?**
- **Will it be the same/different this time?**
- **What would happen if we …?**

For *generalisation*.

- **What always seems to happen?**
- **Can you see the connection between …?**
- **Is there a rule for this?**

For *proof* (or at least careful justification).

- **What would you say if I disagreed?**
- **Can you convince me?**
- **Can you show me that it *definitely* will/will not?**

Building these sorts of questions into your teaching will ensure that children are learning not just mathematical facts, but how to act mathematically. Just as importantly it makes mathematics more enjoyable too, as Joe and Chris found out in sticking up for their ideas about sequences in the case study.

But is all this possible for younger children? Well, imagine a group of Year 1 pupils who are learning to count-on 10 from a number. We might simply teach this as a 'skill' by practising it again and again until they can do it reliably. But instead, imagine asking them to add ten to some numbers ending in 2 (42, 62, etc.) and then asking for *conjectures*. We might ask them to 'guess what will happen with 72', to predict what would happen if we began with a number ending in three (say 43) instead, and so on. From this, they might begin to *generalise* by articulating 'what always happens' and creating a rule (in words) for it. We could leave it there, but it becomes more interesting still if we challenge them to stand up for their mathematical ideas. We might deliberately say we disagree and ask them to convince us. With this kind of approach, it is not just about *learning that* ...; it is about thinking and testing out *what might*, considering *how and why* it does and standing up for our *right to say so*. Notice, too, that it will not work if you put the objective: 'To know that adding ten to a number alters the tens digit by one' on the board at the start. The lesson needs an air of mystery, so keep the objective until the end. Heresy!

Making maths work around national strategies

We noted above that the case study we presented was deliberately set as a whole-day event. On one level we hope that the way you might reorganise this into a series of lessons is obvious. You could tackle one part of the sequence of tasks each day, building up the mathematical thinking as you go over the course of a week or more. At another level though it raises a number of issues that we consider to be limitations of the current system (in England at least) which has packaged mathematics into daily lessons in three parts. Though we cannot deal in depth with these here, we suggest you might consider the points under 'To think about' as you plan your maths teaching.

TO THINK ABOUT
TO THINK ABOUT

If you want to make your maths teaching more centred on problematic and puzzling contexts, how do the following issues affect what you do?

- Problem-solving in the current national numeracy strategy relates almost entirely to *word* problems. To what extent is this a useful form for children?

- The focus of national strategies has been on competence and fluency in numerical calculation. Though important, does this particular focus dominate too much?

- Does the tight, three-part lesson structure promoted by the numeracy strategy militate against both extended thinking and children's autonomy?

- Learning objectives in the strategy are far more likely to relate to conceptual objects (such as addition or properties of shape) than to problem-solving processes. How can we change this balance?

- The strategy dictates that 'good teaching' should have pace, a high proportion of direct teaching and explanation, demonstration and so on. How do these fit with the thinking time and open-endedness that children need for problems? Can it allow children to be creative?

Conclusion

To do mathematics you need facts and skills, just as a musician needs scales and technique to play well and to enjoy doing so. But maths is not, itself, simply a collection of these facts and skills; you have to *do* it. We hope that this chapter has offered an insight into three key aspects of this 'doing'.

- The need to have something problematic to work on (there is no maths without something initially unknown to think about) and the potential for the mathematical and the real worlds to stimulate each other.

- **The way in which numerical, geometric and graphical/pictorial work complement each other by providing different insights into the same idea.**
- **Key aspects of the *discipline* of maths which help learners to think and act mathematically.**

The joy of mathematics comes from overcoming challenges, seeing new insights and patterns and being challenged in your thinking. Children (and adults) will enjoy it most when they begin to see how mathematical ways of thinking, and the structure of the subject itself, provide not just a tool for practical situations but also an authoritative voice which is empowering and creative. That the tens digit increases by one when you add ten, or that the sum of the internal angles on a plane triangle add up to 180° is true, not because the teacher says so, but because the structure of the mathematics dictates it. This fact means that the 'right' to say that something works (to prove it) comes not from the teacher but *from the mathematics itself*. This kind of thinking is empowering, exciting, democratic, creative and, once you get the idea, joyful!

Further reading

Devon County Council (Primary Mathematics Team) (2005) *Using and Applying in Every Maths Lesson: Ideas for the Primary Classroom.* Exeter: DCS Publications.
A very practical guide to making maths lessons more thoughtful. Each of the objectives of the National Numeracy Strategy is rewritten as an investigative question. Ideal for helping teachers to frame maths work as investigative and problematic.

Pratt, N. (2006) *Interactive Maths Teaching in the Primary School.* London: Paul Chapman Publishing.
A guide to making mathematics teaching engaging for pupils by developing strategies for making them think mathematically and in more depth. Practical ideas are included, but these are founded on a close consideration of what mathematics, and teaching mathematics, is all about.

References

Boaler, J. (2002) *Experiencing School Mathematics: Traditional and Reform Approaches to Teaching and Their Impact on Student Learning.* London: Erlbaum.
Paulos, J.A. (2000) *Innumeracy: Mathematical Illiteracy and Its Consequences.* London: Penguin.
Stewart, I. (1997) *The Magical Maze: Seeing the World Through Mathematical Eyes.* London: Phoenix.

13
Joyful teaching and learning in science
Rachael Hincks

Introduction

It would have been quite easy to write a whole book about how joyful science teaching and learning is. However, in order to write a single chapter I have had to consider the fundamental elements, leading me to question why pupils need to learn science and, consequently, the reason for teaching science at all.

I also considered my own exposure to science in the classroom as a child. What features of science education do I remember and why? My first memories of being excited about science are from watching Johnny Ball on BBC television, *Think of a Number*, and deciding that I wanted either to be on his programme or to have his job. It was the infectious nature of his love of science that drew me in, and the way in which he brought the subject to life. I also remember this being very significant in my enjoyment of being a pupil in science lessons in school. I wanted to know more, to ask questions, to think creatively and to investigate.

The world of science is always changing, leading to moral, ethical, social and political debate. As we try to prepare future citizens in our classrooms it is the exploration of science which adds to pupils' understanding of the world around them. Science is also about how things work, how we work, and why this is so. It is about experimentation, exploring new ideas and looking again at explanations we might have once accepted as fact. Science education, as I view it, is about asking questions.

Background

Science is and should be fascinating; as a subject of study it is built on the human fascination with why and how things do what they do or appear how they appear. The QCA science scheme of work for Key Stages 1 and 2 (QCA, 2000) states that children should be curious about things they observe, and experience and explore the world about them with all their senses. As teachers, we are responsible for fostering excitement and encouraging pupils to actively engage with their own learning. Pupils will respond enthusiastically to a teacher who naturally shows the love they have for a subject, as well as the necessary knowledge of it. We all too often expect pupils to answer *our* questions, rather than allowing them to ask their questions and develop their own thoughts and ideas.

Science is about real life; it is about the world around us. For some reason we can easily forget this and present a dry and boring subject that has no connection to pupils' experiences and interests. Gura (1994) discusses the importance of *the need for learning to be situated in contexts which offer worthwhile experience, in accessible forms from children's as well as adults' perspectives* (p133). Again, making the curriculum relevant will only enhance pupils' enjoyment of science and therefore have an impact on progress in the subject.

Asking and answering questions

Children are naturally inquisitive and many parents encourage and develop this inclination from an early age. One of the joys of teaching science is listening to children asking questions – questions about things that we as adults may never think about questioning and might not even know the answers to. Think back to your own childhood and the questions you may have confused your parents with, such as 'why is the sky blue?' or 'how does that aeroplane stay up?' The great inventor Thomas Alva Edison asked so many questions as a child that his teachers despaired of him and he had to be educated at home.

Many children become afraid of putting their hand up in class for fear of getting the answer wrong. As we know, there are often no 'right answers' in science. For example, who still believes the world is flat or that the Earth is the only planet? If children have had negative experiences of asking or answering questions, it becomes much more difficult to encourage those pupils to participate and to become confident in asking or answering questions again, something of which all teachers should be aware.

When children ask questions, it is important to give them your time in terms of exploring the answer to that question. Sometimes it is appropriate for you to give a direct answer, other times it may be much more beneficial to the whole class to allow a discussion of possible answers and reasons for those answers.

ACTION POINT ACTION POINT ACTION POINT ACTION POINT ACTION POINT

> Pose open-ended as well as closed questions, both in discussion and in written tasks. Use terms such as 'what if?', 'explain how ...' or 'give an example of', rather than just: 'What is ...?'

Who, what, when, where and why are all interrogative pronouns used to find answers to questions. Using a combination of these words when considering answers will provide much more meaningful learning opportunities for children and give them a deeper understanding of concepts and ideas. These words can be used to probe pupils' answers to gauge their level of understanding and to develop ideas further.

When children answer questions, it is important to give time to consider their answer and not to dismiss 'wrong' answers. Give enough time for pupils to organise their answers and give a considered response. Ensure that all members of the class are given the opportunity to respond, not always taking answers from the same pupils.

Do not forget to differentiate questions according to ability or by outcome in terms of the length or depth of response. Again, this can be applied to discussion work as well as written tasks. Questioning should challenge all pupils, the most able as well as the least.

Teachers have a varied toolkit of strategies they can use. Consider the position of your body in the classroom – move closer to those who do not easily respond to questions or come down to eye level to make pupils feel more comfortable. Using games such as a quiz show format can make questioning more fun.

ACTION POINT ACTION POINT ACTION POINT ACTION POINT ACTION POINT

> Use an interactive whiteboard to develop interesting questioning games. Display a timer to show children how long they have left to answer the question, with colourful graphics to hold their attention. A fun idea is to display pictures of the pupils – a photo of a child selected at random could be displayed up on the board to show whose turn it is to answer the question. This can also be used as a team exercise.

Children leading their own learning

To engage children fully in science, they should be given opportunities to develop their own ideas and to lead their own learning. Encourage children to think about what they already know, e.g. by using concept maps, but also to consider what they would like to know. You could begin a topic by reviewing the previous year/term's work using a concept map then ask them in groups to come up with questions they would like to find answers to and ways in which they could extend their learning. Not all activities need to be teacher-led.

Key Quote

From a Year 6 pupil: *I think that pupils do practical science at school because they can find things out for themselves rather than the teacher telling them. It's more fun than just the teacher showing them.* (Cited in Braund and Driver, 2005)

Investigations in science can provide ideal opportunities for pupils to take control, leading and promoting their own learning. Another of the joys of teaching and learning in science for most teachers comes from watching children discover something for themselves.

CASE STUDY 13.1

Circuit making

A class of Year 4 pupils were given a selection of equipment including insulated (plastic-coated) wires, bulbs, bulb holders and batteries and the task of 'making the bulb light up'. When they were in Year 2, all of the pupils had covered this topic and some had already made mild protestations about how they had done the work before. The teacher, however, was concerned that their previous exposure to circuits was highly structured and wanted the children to develop a deeper understanding of the electricity topic. In this task they were not given circuit boards and crocodile clips; the teacher wanted to see if they could still light up the bulb without these.

It was interesting to watch the pupils becoming unsure about what they were doing and realising that the current would not flow through the plastic coating on the wire. A short plenary ('all together') was conducted partway through the lesson and the teacher asked the children questions about what was happening. The children responded but also asked probing questions about why the circuits would not work; they shared their prior knowledge about what they had discovered and finally discussed how they could try and make it work now.

A few of the children found that instead of wrapping the insulated wire around the bulb holder, they could make the bulb light up by touching the end of the wire to it. They speculated about what materials made up the insulated wire and what part needed to be touching the bulb holder for the current to flow. This was widened out into a discussion about electrical conductors and insulators.

Finally, the children returned to their circuit making and discovered that the plastic coating needed to be stripped from the ends of the wires before wrapping the wire around the connectors of the bulb holder. They were really excited that the bulbs finally lit up.

Conducting the investigation in this way gave a sense of empowerment to the less able pupils in realising that even the most able pupils did not know how to complete the circuit straightaway and were not necessarily the first to figure it out. The enquiry-based approach allowed all pupils to take ownership of their learning and to work independently, considering their ideas and finding their own routes forward, supported through the discussion of these ideas with their peers.

TO THINK ABOUT

Consider introducing practical work without telling children the final outcome, as investigations are often too structured and do not allow children to follow their own lines of enquiry and explore their own ideas. Alternatively, children could just be faced with a selection of equipment and a question to answer, rather than a step-by-step method. This exploratory approach gives children the ability to get things wrong and to try again – too often as teachers we seem scared to let children simply try things out.

Dealing with misconceptions

Science teaching should build upon a child's existing knowledge or ideas. As Taiwo et al. (1999) state: *Children do not come to science classes with tabula rasa ['blank slate'] minds about science concepts. They come to school already equipped with some understanding, pseudo-knowledge, or misconceptions about science* (p413). Children *will* have misconceptions; they *will* get the answer wrong. While it is important to deal with misconceptions, this does not need to happen straightaway or at the beginning of a lesson. Children will often find their way through a problem and iron out misconceptions as they go, so encourage discussion about why a child has given that answer and why they think the way they do.

ACTION POINT ACTION POINT ACTION POINT ACTION POINT ACTION POINT

> A common misconception is around the difference between dissolving and disappearing. Children will often say that the salt has disappeared when it is stirred into water. Rather than explain the difference between dissolving and disappearing straightaway, you could encourage them to come up with tests that can help them decide if the salt has gone or if it is still there, e.g. by boiling and filtering, by tasting (consider health and safety first).

Misconceptions also provide a good opportunity for more able pupils to lead the learning in explaining why something might not be so. Fostering a safe and welcoming classroom climate will empower pupils to feel able to discuss others' answers or to receive constructive comments. Some misconceptions are very common and it is important that you, the teacher, are aware of these and can build in strategies to discuss them as well as anticipating some of the trickier questions pupils may ask.

TO THINK ABOUT

Pupils often assume that if an object is wrapped up it will keep warm, and do not always understand that wrapping will also keep something cold. Children can discover this for themselves by being allowed to experiment with different materials being wrapped around beakers of cold liquids as well as hot.

TO THINK ABOUT

TO THINK ABOUT

- Over 40 per cent of body heat can be lost through the head (by not wearing a hat).

- A giraffe has the same number of bones in its neck as a human.

- Pumice is a rock that actually floats.

- There is no gravity at the centre of the earth – it all cancels out.

- The total length of all the blood vessels in the human body is about 97,000 km – this is over twice the circumference of the Earth.

(Planet Science, 2006)

Collaborative learning

Encouraging children to work together will enable them to develop transferable skills that are useful both in other areas of the curriculum and outside of school. Skills such as leadership and teamwork can be extended by grouping children and letting them decide upon their own roles in a team in trying to find the answer to a question or deciding upon a route forward with an experiment. Alternatively, you could assign roles to each member of a group, e.g. chairperson, scribe, mentor, reporter.

CASE STUDY 13.2

Designated roles

A class of Year 5 pupils were given a selection of living things and asked to classify them into groups. This often led to arguments, so the teacher arranged the class into groups of four and asked them to decide who would be the chair, the scribe, the mentor and the reporter. The chairperson was able to lead a vote and ask each of the children in the group what their ideas were and how they arrived at them. The scribe took notes for the chairperson which the reporter then used to feedback to the rest of the class during the plenary. The role of the mentor in the group was to remind the pupils of the task and to ensure the task was completed.

During the plenary session, each reporter fed back the ideas from their group, which led on to a whole-class discussion. The task was differentiated by outcome: less able pupils were able to discuss their ideas in basic terms, e.g. animals that live on land or in water, whereas more able pupils discussed their ideas using more sophisticated scientific language, e.g. amphibians, mammals. The pupils enjoyed having a designated role in the group as they all had something to contribute and their input was valued.

Collaborative learning can also enable you to work with most children in the class within each lesson, revisiting and questioning each group. This technique can also aid with classroom management, including keeping pupils on task who might otherwise disrupt the lesson.

Tools such as concept cartoons can be used to encourage group discussion and as a lead-in to practical work. Concept cartoons are an alternative to concept maps and brainstorms and can be used to consolidate learning and to develop further questions.

The example in Figure 13.1 could be given to a class of pupils organised into mixed-ability groups of four. Pupils would look at the pictures and consider the ideas presented, discussing each one and deciding upon possible right answers. This also gives an opportunity to elicit misconceptions and to reassure pupils that others might share their ideas.

Figure 13.1 Concept cartoon
Source: Naylor and Keogh (2000); reproduced with permission.

Conclusion

It is easy to assume that science is a difficult or technical subject because of the vocabulary used or the way in which the subject itself is presented. However, the teaching and learning of science can indeed be a very joyous experience – the rewards are in seeing pupils genuinely find things out for themselves and willingly share their ideas with others. The enjoyment or love of a subject is a huge motivator for the children in your class and something which will hopefully lead to a path of lifelong learning.

Key Quote
OK, so what's the speed of dark? (Steven Wright)

Further reading

Farrow, S. (2006) *The Really Useful Science Book: A Framework of Knowledge for Primary Teachers*. Abingdon and New York: Routledge.
This book contains all you need to know about science teaching and learning.

Harlen, W. (ed.) (2006) *ASE Guide to Primary Science Education*. Hatfield: Association for Science Education.
An easy-to-read book with interesting chapters about issues such as the purpose of science education and a handy reference guide for all trainee primary teachers.

Peacock, G., Sharp, J., Johnsey, R. and Wright, D. (2007) *Primary Science: Knowledge and Understanding*. Exeter: Learning Matters.
A comprehensive guide to teaching science, containing lots of practical examples and tips for in the classroom.

References

Braund, M. and Driver, M. (2005) Pupils' perceptions of practical science in primary and secondary school: implications for improving progression and continuity of learning. *Educational Research*, 47 (1), 77–91.

Gura, P. (1994) Scientific and technological development in the Early Years, in G.M. Blenkin and A.V. Kelly (1994) *The National Curriculum and Early Learning: An Evaluation*. London: Paul Chapman Publishing.

Naylor, S. and Keogh, B. (2000) *Concept Cartoons in Science Education*. Crewe: Millgate House Publishing.

Planet Science (2006) Available online at: http://www.scienceyear.com.

QCA (2000) *Science: A Scheme of Work for Key Stages 1 and 2*. London: Qualifications and Curriculum Authority.

Taiwo, A.A., Ray, H., Motswiri, M.J. and Masene, R. (1999) Perceptions of the water cycle among primary school children in Botswana. *International Journal of Science Education*, 21 (4), 413–29.

14
The joy of meeting pupil needs through developing community
Suanne Gibson and Helen Knowler

Introduction

This chapter provides academic and practical insights regarding meeting the needs of all pupils, doing so in ways that are meaningful both for you and pupils, while at the same time maintaining a focus on academic excellence and achievement for your school. The first part introduces you to contemporary policy and practice issues in relation to inclusion and mainstream education. The second part provides a breakdown on the development of government policy and academic research in the area of inclusion and its impact upon the teacher. The third part unpacks the concept of school as community and its importance in the effective provision of learning and teaching for all pupils regardless of need. The final part provides insight through practical case study examples of effective and inclusive education practices. Community lies at the heart of life both inside and outside the school. Staff in school, outside agencies and parents working together are the hope for the future, so read on with expectation.

Background

Since 1994 in England and as reflected throughout much of the world, inclusive thinking, particularly with regard to the education of children labelled with disability, has become prominent in education policy and practice. Supporters of this mode of education base their ideals and values on social justice and views of a liberal humanitarian society. The aim of an inclusive education policy is that education becomes accessible to and for all and in so doing is both a positive and developmental experience. Recent developments in education policy reflect this thinking, with an emphasis on inclusive education, where all children, regardless of need, disability, gender, cultural background, class and geographical location, can and should be educated together. As Slee (2001) comments:

> Inclusive schooling is a greater challenge than is implied [...] in the technical attempts to mobilise sufficient resources to contain disabled children in incrementally modified classrooms. (p116)

Education documents confirm the government's policy commitment to enhancing educational standards for all pupils. The 1999 Green Paper depicts the government's definition of inclusion (DfEE, 1999, p44):

> Inclusion is a process, not a fixed state. By Inclusion we mean not only that pupils with SEN [special educational needs] should wherever possible receive their education in a mainstream school, but that they should fully join with their peers in the curriculum and life of the school [...] rather than be isolated in special units.

The key argument being made in this chapter is that to be effective in meeting the learning needs of all your pupils, to address your continuing professional development (CPD) needs, to locate yourself within the school as an inclusive teacher and to be enabled to critically evaluate your practices, you need to draw on a community. We do not function in isolation; in our endeavours to make the curriculum accessible and the classroom functional we need to draw on the wisdom, experiences, support and input of others, e.g. teachers, the special educational needs co-ordinator (SENCO), teaching assistants, parents and pupils.

TO THINK ABOUT

- The teacher does not function as an isolated individual responsible only for his or her pupils' learning.

- Your professional knowledge develops over time and through experience.

Key Quote
Inclusive thinking is steeped in philosophies of social justice and human rights discourse.
(Gibson, 2006, p325)

History of special educational needs provision

Children have their own unique talents, abilities and strengths. One of the biggest challenges that you will face in the primary classroom is how to meet the diverse educational, social and emotional skills of the children we teach.

Primary school teachers have always had to work with a variety of abilities and learning needs; however, for the last thirty years the support given to children with SEN (sometimes called Additional Learning Needs, ALN) has been debated, contested and changed in the light of high-profile research reports, research evidence and policy development.

The Warnock Report of 1978 radically changed the way that children with SEN are supported in schools. Prior to 1978 the group of children deemed to be of lower ability were classified in a variety of ways, including 'educationally subnormal', 'backward' or 'slow learners'. The expectations for these children were not particularly high since it was assumed that it would be virtually impossible for them to overcome the barriers to learning they faced daily. Teachers were encouraged to support them in the best way that they could, but it was generally accepted that to meet the needs of children at this ability level was something only a 'specialist' teacher could do.

The Warnock Report led to legislation that removed explicit categorisation of children, but instead talked about special educational needs that might be met in mainstream classrooms. This policy promoted a move towards integration rather than segregation, meaning that children with a variety of learning needs could now access staff and resources in a setting alongside their peers. It also prompted the expectation that any suitably qualified teacher could work with children with a range of needs to support their educational and emotional development.

Throughout the 1980s and early 1990s the experiences of children with SEN very much depended on the staff, resources and systems within each local education authority. The introduction of the Special Educational Needs Code of Practice in 1994 required that schools should have staff with responsibility for the co-ordination of special needs provision, that they identify the needs of individuals and that they attempt to meet the needs of those individuals as much as possible within their own setting. The updated Special Educational Needs Code of Practice 2001 incorporated the introduction of the SEN and Disability Act 2001, which prohibits schools from discriminating against disabled children in their admission arrangements.

A commitment to the principles of Inclusive Education was reflected in the revised National Curriculum in 2000 which contained an Inclusion Statement, clearly outlining the responsibility of all teachers to meet the needs of all learners. The document outlines three broad principles as essential for developing an 'inclusive curriculum'.

- **setting suitable learning challenges;**
- **responding to pupils' diverse learning needs;**
- **overcoming barriers to learning and assessment for individuals and groups of pupils.**

The notion that all teachers can play a role in the education of children with SEN was further emphasised in the 2004 publication, *Removing Barriers to Achievement: The Government's Strategy for Special Educational Needs*. This document sets out a vision for all children to reach their full potential regardless of ability and to protect the right to a good education with access to the same learning opportunities as other learners. It highlights the importance of early intervention and the role that you play in removing barriers to learning, whatever they may be. In line with the Every Child Matters document of 2005, *Removing Barriers* stresses the importance of well-matched and timely interventions to secure positive outcomes for the individual.

There have been many changes in the way that children with SEN are perceived, labelled and supported over the last three decades. The legislation that has recently been introduced is intended to protect the rights of children with SEN to be fully included as members of a school community, to receive a broad and balanced education and to be subject to the same high standards and expectations as others.

TO THINK ABOUT

- How can I ensure that I am meeting the needs of individual learners?

- How can I ensure that in my planning, teaching and assessment I am actively seeking to remove barriers to achievement?

- How can I ensure that I am getting the support I need?

- What are my continuing professional development needs?

Key Quote

Disability is a complex form of social oppression or institutionalised discrimination [...] theoretical analysis has shifted from individuals and their impairment to disabling environments and hostile attitudes. (Barnes,1996, p1)

Inclusive education is [...] an approach which requires both increasing participation and the removal of barriers to radical school reform. (Allan, 2000, p1)

Responding to individual need therefore becomes the responsibility of the primary or secondary school community, i.e. the school adapting its environment, teaching practices and policy to meet and manage effectively all pupil needs.

School and community

It is important to take into consideration the role and place of the local community, its impact as well as involvement in the establishing of inclusive school communities. Schools and their local communities do not exist in isolation from each other and for effective learning and teaching to take place there need to be meaningful connections established, e.g. home–school partnerships, schools working closely with national programmes such as Connexions (for older pupils) and Sure Start (for pre-school and primary). Once these community partnerships have been established and effective communication enabled within and between them a basis is formed from where an inclusive school community can emerge.

Case study 14.1 depicts a school and local community working together to enable a more inclusive way of teaching pupils with SEN, taking the local community into consideration and utilising this as an effective resource. The study is drawn from work by Gibson (2006) which focused in part on the role of community in supporting inclusive developments in schools.

CASE STUDY 14.1

Removing barriers

The following extract tells a story of the inclusive teaching and learning ideas which emerged when dialogue occurred between and within various levels and groups of a school community. It depicts innate processes of exclusion at various levels of the education system which stand as barriers to innovative ideas being realised. It is an extract taken from an interview with the deputy head teacher who had been seconded by the local authority due to the school's inspection failure. The deputy head teacher commented:

We were put on Special Measures due to low attainment, poor pupil behaviour, low attendance, poor Special Educational Needs and poor management. The kids at our school are very needy kids; they come from a problem area. The SENCO, working closely with our teachers, TAs, the parents and their children has set up a family learning programme to have mums involved in teaching their kids; only a half are involved. It is due to a mixture of apathy, low community self-esteem, disorganisation, and a hang-up that many of the parents have from their own school days.

The language used denotes a negative tale, a picture of failure and also of acceptance of the status quo, where it is assumed there are causal links between 'needy kids', 'problem areas' and 'educational failure'. There is also a sense of the positive of a community working together, listening to the voices of parents, pupils and teachers in their attempts to rejuvenate their school community.

As is apparent from Case study 14.1, schools and their local communities need each other in order to function effectively and inclusively. As a teacher you will not be working alone but with others: teaching colleagues, teaching assistants, pupils, school governors and, ideally, parents. In order for these interactions to be managed effectively and efficiently it is ideal that a school has a team responsible, i.e. an SEN management committee with representation from teachers, SENCOS, teaching assistants, parents and pupils. In practice such a committee should work together in compiling a school inclusion/SEN policy to guide the school in its aims and objectives. Community participation is imperative in establishing ownership and legitimacy of such a policy.

Of course the underlying assumption is that those involved will feel confident in the task required; thus it is important that you as a new teacher are given opportunities to address your professional abilities and needs. The 'To think about' box below offers a series of questions that you need to address in order to assess your capabilities and needs in this area of practice.

TO THINK ABOUT

- Have you had the opportunity to shadow a colleague and/or observe a visiting expert?
- Have you had a chance for involvement in any team teaching with colleagues and/or teaching assistants?
- Have you ever been involved in a community initiative involving colleagues, pupils, youth workers, teaching assistants, LA and/or parents?
- How are you and/or could you be involved in the school community that extends beyond the school as 'institution'?

The academic insights and case study example above emphasise the importance of 'community', the benefits of having fostered a community approach to education within and throughout the school environment. It is on this basis that your role as part of this community will emerge but it cannot do so without support, guidance and regular evaluation and this is where the role of the tutor or mentor will be important.

Contemporary research into practitioner practices and thinking in education reveal a highly favoured view of inclusion (Croll and Moses, 2003). Most teachers believe the best place for all children, regardless of who or what they are, is learning together, and this is reflected in practitioner publications. While the philosophy and ideals behind inclusion in meeting the needs of all learners are in the main supported by teachers there is a continuing need for professional input and guidance to support effective practice.

CASE STUDY 14.2

Fresh start

Our second case study is an example of how a school planned the managed transfer of a pupil with social, emotional and behavioural difficulties from another primary school. The teacher responsible for co-ordinating the move explains how she worked to ensure that the move was well planned and that everyone in the school community can work together to make the move a successful transition in the life of a vulnerable pupil:

In a staff meeting, our head teacher told us that he had been approached about a 'managed move'. He explained that the boy, called Dan, was at risk of exclusion in his own school and that it was now thought to be a good idea if he had a fresh start in a new school.

As his potential new teacher the first thing I did was to go to his old school and meet Dan's present class teacher, who did not hesitate to describe his poor behaviour, not helped by the fact that he did not have a statement of his needs and the school could barely spare any teaching assistant support for him. However, his teacher did say that he loved helping people and was really good with younger children. He was poor in literacy and numeracy, but enjoyed reading with younger learners. He was mad about football and PE and was also good at computers.

The head teacher asked me to think about a reward scheme and appropriate sanctions. I made a lunchtime and playtime plan so that every day there was something for him to do and it was not left to chance that he would just have to get on with it. I had a meeting with all mealtime assistants to explain the background and to talk to them about the importance of nurturing positive relationships. We discussed a manageable timetable of activities and places for him to go each lunchtime and we devised a three-week rolling programme so there was something different for him to do each week.

I met with the teaching assistants and talked about the shared responsibility of all staff. Everyone had a job to help him settle in and to remind him of our school agreements. We wrote scripts so that we would all be talking to him in a similar way and our expectations were clear and achievable. We went through a clear exit procedure when things go wrong and what to do to ensure that all children were kept safe. I made sure that everyone knew about his rewards and sanctions and told them that I wanted everyone to work in that way for consistency.

I then spent some time talking to the children in the class to tell them about the boy, Dan. I wanted to prepare them and so I took time to revisit our classroom agreements. I talked about how poor behaviour can be a barrier to learning. We discussed the fact that it meant that they would have to learn strategies for helping Dan learn how to behave in an appropriate way.

Finally, in the week before Dan arrived I ran an informal parents session where I invited parents to come in and hear about our new arrival. The head and I talked at length about our inclusive ethos and the ways we intended to support this child. We asked for their support and talked about the rewards and sanction systems that we would adopt.

TO THINK ABOUT
TO THINK ABOUT

- Case study 14.2 highlights the importance of good communication between all members of the school community in order to meet the complex needs of an individual.

- In what ways did the class teacher work to ensure communication was effective?

- How many people were spoken to about the managed moved?

- How did the teacher work to ensure she was supported effectively?

- In what way did the teacher take responsibility for preparing appropriate provision?

Creative approaches and practicalities

Many teachers will tell you that most of the strategies recommended for teaching children with SEN are in fact suitable for most, if not all, pupils. One of the most important things you can do when you are new to a school is to find out about the approaches they take to working with and supporting pupils with SEN. The school will most probably have built up effective practice around particular areas and you will have a lot to learn from this.

There is much you can do on a personal level to ensure that you are developing, supporting and encouraging a sense of community in your own classroom and with the children you work with. You should consider the ways in which the classroom itself can be a barrier to learning. Very often how pupils are seated and the groups they are placed in can impact on their work and achievement. You should look for ways to support learning and progress by considering your seating plans carefully. This might include areas for collaborative and individual work, areas for quiet work and calming zones should pupils require 'time out' out from busy classroom life. You need to ensure that you have established effective and simple routines so that every pupil (and not just those with SEN) understands what is expected of them in the learning environment. Think carefully about display – this can be a powerful tool in helping children with SEN to gain a sense of independence and develop problem-solving skills. Pretty classrooms look nice, but think about the way display could reduce barriers to participation. For example, instead of relying on verbal instructions for classroom routines, use pictures to show children what they need to do to be ready for learning.

Recognising individual achievement is a crucial factor in supporting children with SEN. The current climate whereby SATs scores are sometimes valued above all other forms of achievement can result in an emphasis on what children cannot do, rather than highlighting all that they can. An extremely important element of your role will be to recognise, record and monitor achievement for the individual. You should take every opportunity to celebrate success with the children in your class, with the whole school, with parents and with the entire school community to develop the sense that every person in the school makes a valuable contribution to the success of the school. There are a number of practical things that you can do to support children with SEN that will also benefit other members of the class.

- **Praise, encourage and reward whenever possible to show that you recognise and value the achievement of *all* pupils.**
- **Allow time for children with SEN to complete tasks. It is tempting to rattle through curriculum content, but everyone likes to feel they have finished something to the best of their ability.**
- **Use a variety of teaching approaches and do not be afraid to experiment. It is good practice to use lots of different ways to explain the same thing. This goes someway to ensuring that all children have access to the curriculum and an opportunity to participate fully within the learning opportunity.**
- **Always think carefully about evidence for learning – not everything has to be a written outcome and it is important that children with SEN get to show their achievements in a variety of ways.**
- **Practise your approaches to questioning and explaining and giving regular feedback to children.**

ACTION POINTS ACTION POINTS ACTION POINTS ACTION POINTS ACTION POINTS

Spend time with colleagues responsible for SEN/disability in your school and talk to them about the approaches the school has found to be successful with individuals. As you do so, carry out the following.

> **Discover how you will get access to the training and development you might need to support individuals in your own classroom.**

> **Find out the name of the educational psychologist and, if possible, ask him or her about specialist services.**

> **Learn how provision is managed in your school for the different types of SEN. For example, how is provision organised for pupils with social, emotional and behavioural difficulties or speech and communication difficulties?**

> **Key Quote**
> *There are no magic formulae or extra-special curricular devices which have to be used with chil-dren who experience difficulties. There is no need to assume that certain special teaching styles or strategies are only accessible to those who have had long training or experience. The main requirement is for creativity and imagination to make the curriculum come alive for all children.*
> (Thomas, Walker and Webb, 1998, p6)

Conclusion

This chapter has endeavoured to support you in understanding developments in educa-tion policy and practice that promote a more positive view of different learners and learning styles. We have also made some supportive suggestions on ways in which you can implement this inclusive thinking into your teaching practices and address any related CPD needs.

Schools and their communities need to allow resources, giving time and space for teach-ers to share views, feelings and experiences in relation to inclusive education. This should ideally occur in a supportive environment as colleague interaction and peer sup-port can and, where managed effectively, do lead to progressive educational practices and deeper understandings regarding inclusive education.

Part of the reason that many people become primary teachers is because they want to help children who, for one reason or another, are struggling with school life. The ideas and suggestions provided in this chapter give you a joyous opportunity to do just that.

Further reading

Gibson, S. and Blandford, S. (2005) *Managing Special Educational Needs: A Practical Guide for Primary and Secondary Schools*. London: Paul Chapman Publishing.
Contains a wealth of ideas and guidance on how to manage an inclusive school environment, with practical solutions to the everyday problems encountered by busy teachers.

Gross, J. (2002) *Special Educational Needs in the Primary School: A Practical Guide*. Buckingham: Open University Press.
A very clearly written guide with lots of advice, ideas and information on supporting children with special educational needs. The book can be read cover to cover but it is equally good to dip into for inspiration.

Hayward, A. (2006) *Making Inclusion Happen: A Practical Guide*. London: Paul Chapman Publishing.
This book is easy to read and understand, offering a clear view of inclusion. It contains a range of practical materials that will help you to develop your own inclusive practice.

References

Allan, J. (2000) *It's Good to Talk: Bridging the Gap Between Disability Studies and Inclusive Education*, ISEC 2000 CD ROM. Oldham: Inclusive Consultancy and Training Ltd.
Barnes, C. (1996) *Disabling Imagery and the Media*. Leeds: Disability Press.
Croll, P. and Moses, D. (2003) Special educational needs across two decades: survey evidence from English primary schools. *British Educational Research Journal*, 29 (5), 697–713.

Department for Education and Employment (1999) *Meeting Special Educational Needs: A Programme of Action*. London: DfEE.

Department for Education and Skills (2004) *Removing Barriers to Achievement: The Government's Strategy for Special Educational Needs*. London: DfES.

Gibson, S. (2006) Beyond a culture of silence: inclusive education and the liberation of voice. *Disability and Society*, 21 (4), 315–29.

Slee, R. (2001) Inclusion in practice: does practice make perfect? *Educational Review*, 53 (2), 113–22.

Thomas, G., Walker, D. and Webb, J. (1998) *The Making of the Inclusive School*. Abingdon: Routledge.

15
Seat yourselves joyfully together
Jeff Lewis

Introduction

The title of this chapter is taken from the Babylonian creation epic.

The recent success of the internet phenomenon 'Friends Reunited' indicates that those with whom we shared our schooling remain important to us over an extended period. Some, of course, have only painful memories of being bullied or ostracised, while others may be carrying rose-tinted nostalgic images of a reality that was perhaps not so enchanting. Nevertheless, many of our positive memories of school concern being engaged as part of a group or community and sharing something of importance in our development as a person. It is likely that many of these instances will concern extra-curricular events rather than classroom learning, where all too often we sat on our own, struggling with content that eluded our understanding but, apparently, not that of some of our classmates. If only, we felt, we could have talked to them and achieved a glimpse of the insights they clearly had, but that would have been seen as cheating. This chapter concerns the power of learning together, of how this may be facilitated and of how its engagement may lead to the experience of a real and lasting joy.

Friendships and joy in learning

I will assume throughout this chapter that a group (e.g. a class in school) is enriched by an experience of mutual friendship, and that this experience is indeed joyful. By friendship, I am not suggesting that everyone is equally close or that we still don't have special friends or that we go out of our way to be 'nice' or 'happy' together. Rather, I see friendship in the way it is seen by the Quakers (the Religious Society of Friends), as a way of being together that involves unconditional positive regard and a wish and concern for each other's well-being ... you can be friendly to people you have yet to meet. This is conveyed by an attitude, often quiet and understated, summarised by the hymn writer Whittier:

To worship rightly is to love each other
Each smile a hymn, each kindly thought a prayer.

This attitude does not depend on the type of overstated expressions of friendship and liking that strike so many as false and drive them back to seclusion rather than into community. Similarly I don't see joy as an expression of happiness or fun (although it is sometimes manifested as such) but rather as a sense of deep connection that is both reassuring and uplifting. This often occurs when an achievement is recognised, especially if the achievement was hard won, and very often when a community shows solidarity in trying circumstances.

CASE STUDY 15.1

Shared understanding

A young teacher is with his Reception class during a class meeting (circle time). The children are relating recent events and articulating the associated feelings. A small girl reports the death last evening of her grandmother. She is clearly upset and somewhat bewildered. She needs some form of acknowledgement and some reassurance, but what can be said that fulfils those needs without denying the authenticity of the girl's feelings? Intuitively, the teacher knows not to jump in and try to make it alright, but at least to hold the quietness and evident sense of concern that pervades the whole room. Just then, a young boy, normally seen as the most troublesome and uncooperative child in the class intervenes. He relates how he felt with his own similar bereavement and how he gradually, but never completely, came to terms with his loss. He connected fully with his classmate, and without denying her present pain offered a hopeful perspective. It could not have been done better. Further quiet reflection was shared by all, and some other sharing and well-wishing occurred before the class returned to their ordinary activities. A class had now been transformed in their understanding of themselves and each other, with a young teacher inspired by the powerful example of caring that had been manifested before his eyes.

Getting to know you

It is difficult to feel many positive emotions, let alone joy, in a group where you feel uncertain of your place, feel that you are not accepted, or where you are afraid of revealing anything but the most obvious aspects of your being. Every teacher and student teacher I have met has recognised the importance of learning their pupils' names. The strategies with which they accomplish this feat are often ingenious (especially in the case of those who claim to be bad at remembering names) but are often covert or even devious, and only rarely do they involve the pupils themselves in an active learning experience. They seem to assume that the pupils will all know each other and that they are the only ones who need to learn about the class. The fact that they have probably sat for years in seminar and lecture groups where they did not even know everyone's name and only really knew a handful of people – that they normally sat near for comfort and safety – should alert them to the fact that getting to know each other to the extent that everyone is at least comfortable when working with other members of the group cannot be left to chance.

An Education Studies student working as a teaching assistant wrote the following in an assignment, contrasting her experience in a university class with the experience of the class that she was working with in school:

> *I have developed the opinion that not enough emphasis is put on group bonding at the beginning of each school year. I say this because apart from some badly orchestrated circle time, I have never witnessed the large-scale group bonding sessions that we underwent at university at the beginning of our group work module. Within three sessions I felt I belonged there and could work collaboratively with any member of the group. I don't believe I see that in the class I work in at present and most of these children have been together for two and a half years. The truth of the matter is that I am more likely to see rudeness or hostility aimed at classmates rather than trust and compassion. Very often I hear comments like, 'I am not sitting next to him!' or 'I am not working with her!' In fact just the other day a child called across the table to another child, 'What are you looking at?' Does this sound like an environment conducive to learning?*

Naming activities of all sorts need to be used not only at the first meeting (after which it is virtually guaranteed that many names will be forgotten, introducing further barriers fuelled by our embarrassment at having forgotten) but consistently, and to introduce all sorts of activities, whether it be phonics (our names all consist of sounds), numbers (addresses, ages, etc.), maps (we all live somewhere) and so on. For a wide variety of naming activities see Dyer and Lewis (2001). Also, ensure that the class have the opportunity to be called by the name they choose rather than the name on the register, which may well be different. Some people prefer to be called by their middle name or by a shorter version of their forename. I, for instance, am definitely Jeff, not Jeffrey, a word I associate with being reprimanded when young. Also, once a no put-down rule has been established, encourage the class to introduce their preferred nicknames, as long as the nominee has total power to change their own nickname.

A further development would be to become accustomed to our name spelt backward, and the alter ego we associate with it. I, for instance, would be Yerffej, clearly a bold Saxon warrior! Ensure that all names are learned, used often in a variety of settings and, crucially, with total respect. Teach that our chosen names are important, define us and are precious. They must never be abused. How many of us remember being taunted with rhymes and other corruptions of our name, sometimes by a teacher? It is a great destroyer of trust and has no place in a caring community.

But who are you?

Friends know a little more about each other than names and what can be easily observed. This does not mean that we are all expected to reveal our deepest fears and innermost longings to all and sundry, but it does entail that we are comfortable sharing our commonalities, celebrating our differences and enjoying mutual interests. There are many activities which allow for the appropriate disclosure of likes and dislikes, areas of interest, pastimes, etc., perhaps the most powerful being the child-led lesson. I have often witnessed in classrooms a time slot (15 minutes, say) where a child is invited to prepare a presentation about something of personal interest from outside school. Among the topics might be a collection of badges related to a theme, membership of a society or club, a sporting or cultural pursuit that the family is involved in, or details of a hobby. When witnessing such an event one is soon struck by the interest shown by the class, and the level of questioning and reflection that is elicited. The lack of disruption is also evident, and somewhat of an enigma to the teacher, who feels she or he needs to be constantly alert and vigilant if the children are to be kept on task.

A class that knows each other and their interests at this level are far more likely to bring in resources that another might appreciate, take interest in TV programmes that concern the activities of a friend or generate conversations about a wide range of interests. The children themselves are validated by this level of interest, and develop a secure self-image and healthy levels of self-esteem and self-efficacy. Knowledge and practice of peer tutoring (especially cross-age), peer mediation, buddy systems, response partners and plan–do–review teams are now widespread, but could perhaps be built into all pupils' experience.

At the very least each class deserves a regular special time, perhaps a class meeting, a circle time or a celebration of each other's and their own achievements. Circle time can be a very poor experience unless its aims and nature are understood. Children will often need periods of pair work to rehearse their contributions to the larger group. The voluntary principle must be observed at all times, including you, the teacher who must learn to wait your turn too, and not think you have to respond to each offering. Periods of quiet togetherness need to be gradually encouraged.

Circles of this type become far more powerful when the class is actually in control and chooses both when they need to meet and what about. When trusted, young children can be extraordinarily powerful at sorting out their own agenda, and if the model they have is not about blaming and punishing but about restitution and healing, then the effect is of a deep and trusting connection that is indeed a source of joy.

Everyone is welcome

Exclusion and ostracism are particularly hurtful if a group is well constituted, caring, trusting and fun to be part of. You need to work hard to make your classroom an inclusive environment, which celebrates rather than fears diversity, with strategies to include more people more often. Absolutely basic is a level where everyone is at least comfortable working with anyone else in the group. The more people work together, the more they listen to each other, and the more they come to accept and even like each other. Therefore you need to include a wide range of active listening and learning activities in your teaching, some genuinely co-operative and collaborative tasks in small groups and especially pairs, and a measure of responsibility for all children, so that everyone's gifts can be developed and appreciated.

Great care must be given to how these groups are selected. At first the safest option is totally random allocation. Getting the class to pick teams is a notoriously clumsy thing to do, and for many brings up memories of being the last to be picked, despite doing everything to indicate that you should be next. This practice should be avoided at all costs. Simply asking people to get into pairs is hardly less traumatic for the shy, those who believe no one wants to work with them, or where you have the eternal triangle of three friends, one of whom will be mortally offended and seek revenge if he or she is not the chosen one! Once random allocation has allowed everyone to experience working with everyone else, attribute matching can be used to draw attention to each other's qualities. For example, pair up with:

- **someone you haven't worked with;**
- **someone you haven't spoken to today;**
- **someone you haven't spoken to this week;**
- **someone who has the same colour eyes/hair;**
- **someone who lives in a different area.**

TO THINK ABOUT

Until real trust has been built up it is probably better not to highlight race or gender as an attribute; and forcing a boy to publicly pick a girl may well lead to all sorts of problems, especially if a strictly observed 'no put-down' rule is not yet in place. If anyone has a problem that needs sorting, allow the whole class to be part of the solution, through a circle of friends approach, or through class-wide problem-solving. For instance, if one child is having difficulty going into assembly quietly, this is actually a problem for the whole class, so let them find how many ways they can help their friend get to assembly quietly and on time.

CASE STUDY 15.2

Show of solidarity

In a school for children with learning and behaviour difficulties, the senior class included Sandra, a girl with cerebral palsy. One unfortunate effect of this condition was that she had poor lip control, and would often dribble, making her work book messy. The therapist suggested that she needed to spend time exercising control, and as a strategy asked her to hold a milk straw between her lips while she was writing. A teenage girl is bound to feel self-conscious about this, especially if no one understands why she is doing it. I, as her teacher, needed to make this as easy for her as possible, though at the time I only had a rudimentary knowledge of co-operative group work and problem-solving. I therefore talked to the class – teenagers labelled as having learning and behaviour difficulties – explaining why Sandra would be using the straw and asking them to have forbearance and not to draw attention to it, because it was not nice to make people feel different. After break (we still had milk then) and as a writing task began, these young people, with no input from me, all produced straws and held them between their lips as a sign of solidarity. No one commented, but there was a deep and satisfying sense of connection and an unusually light and spacious feel to the room as we all shared with smiles and eye contact the feeling of doing something worthwhile together. Of course, after a while they tired of this, and so did Sandra, and she continued to dribble, but somehow this difference didn't seem as important as before.

One inspiring attempt to achieve full social inclusion in the classroom is reported by Paley (1992) in her book *You Can't Say 'You Can't Play'*. Here the class were challenged to include everyone by being forbidden to refuse a place in any game to anyone. Gradually the various excuses and strategies of exclusion were aired, for example:

- *But it's only a twosey game;*
- *But she's no good at this;*
- *She can play as long as she only holds the rope/runs to get the ball/isn't 'it', or other unpopular roles.*

These were then used, not to correct people or as a basis for a moralising assembly, but as a discussion of what it was like not to be included and how everyone's needs can be met. Eventually the pupils did not need to be banned from excluding; they learnt to enjoy including. And very joyous it was.

None of us is as smart as all of us

This is not the place to go into a critical review of grouping by ability; suffice it to say that while there may be some advantages for some, sometimes there are problems for most, most of the time. The awful self-fulfilling prophecy of being assigned to the 'dumb' group (it doesn't matter what euphemism you refer to the group by ... everyone knows their status) has probably caused the biggest waste of human potential of any educational strategy.

Some believe there is no better alternative, probably because they have not experienced the power of genuinely co-operative group work. In many classrooms children sit in groups but do not work in groups; rather, individualisation and competition still seem to be the watchwords. In other circumstances group activities are introduced, but the tasks selected do not actually encourage group work.

If a task can be accomplished by the most able doing most of the work while the others watch or get confused, then that is precisely what tends to happen. If the most voluble and confident can make all the decisions, right or wrong, while others fail to contribute their ideas or lose track of the development of the project, then that tends to happen too. Some will be constantly given low-level tasks while others do the important work. All of this is more likely if the group see the task not as an opportunity for learning but as a task of competing with another group, getting it done quickly or seeking teacher approval for the finished product rather than a process.

What needs to happen is that the task must *demand* that each person plays an important role, that everyone needs to participate for success, and that the group have practised listening and thinking skills like turn-taking, listening to everyone, reflective paraphrasing to acknowledge and validate ideas, brainstorming and other involving strategies to explore widely, divergent thinking, connecting disparate ideas and arriving at considered consensus rather than the majority rule of voting. There are many ways of achieving this, but a technique that both helps in group work training and allows genuinely co-operative projects in the classroom is the jigsaw technique (see Action Point and below).

TO THINK ABOUT
TO THINK ABOUT

For ease let us assume a class of 25 pupils. Any more or fewer and you will have to reorganise as appropriate. Divide the class into five *home* groups (five in each). When planning the session develop *five* main points. Also plan a summative activity or assessment activity that requires all five areas to be addressed. The activity could be a quiz or the completion of a poster or a map that the home group as a whole must work on. Make one person in each group responsible for *one* of the areas. It is this person's responsibility to become the expert in this area. Collect the experts from each group into five expert groups of five. Each expert group meets, with the resources you have prepared, and discusses how best to explore the area (perhaps they have a set question) and how best to convey this information to their home group. The experts then return to their home groups and help fill in their part of the jigsaw in the summative/assessment task which, if it is graded, attracts a group grade but no individual grades.

The jigsaw technique

Let's say the session is about the Romans. Select five areas, perhaps transport, religion, cities, the army and food. Each home group has an expert on each, each of whom goes to their 'expert' groups. Here they discuss how to broker their expertise, so they all get to rehearse and be confident in their part. Returning to their home group, with the mantle of expert, they are responsible for teaching the others what is necessary for the completion of the task. They are also the final arbiters of the response to the task. Perhaps a poster has been provided onto which the home group must add information and pictures concerning each area. Even the supposed least able will wear the wonderful mantle of expert, and will be supported by their peers in the expert group should they need it. The pupils have all been necessary and valuable players in an episode of co-operative group learning.

Deepening and extending the learning relationship

When children in a group are comfortable with each other and are not afraid to contribute because fear and ridicule have been superseded, and when a truly inclusive ethos has been established and the group are confident in a range of skills and procedures, then real relationship at the level of learning is possible, and the prospect of what O'Sullivan (1999) calls *transformative learning* beckons. The teacher's role is now rather different. She is a provider of learning experiences and a facilitator of group process. These are honourable and challenging roles. It is not a matter of 'lighting the blue touch paper' and standing back, but it is a matter of knowing when to hand over responsibility and to support another in his or her use of it. It is also an opportunity to enter the experience as a co-learner, as an experienced scout rather than as an arbiter of all knowledge.

In a truly inspiring book, *Tuned In and Fired Up,* Sam Intrator (2003) chronicles powerful learning episodes in an American high school English class. While the content dealt with is appropriate to adolescents, the principles of pedagogy will be applicable to any setting. The high-powered episodes described by Intrator where – in an electric moment when the classroom hums with energy and pupils are wholly engaged in learning and find genuine meaning worth and value in their academic experiences – are not everyday occurrences, but do not need to be. It is probable that we could not deal with constant high intensity and need periods to reflect and consolidate. However, the instances that are described, when the pupils fully relate as humans to the curriculum, often when a child has entered fully into a discussion and modelled commitment and authenticity, and where the teacher is able to let the pupils handle their thoughts and emotions without giving ready-made solutions, are truly electrifying. Every teacher deserves to be present at such an event, and the children will have enduring memories of a powerful shared experience where they realised the full humanity of themselves and each other. Sam Intrator's gift is that he has both indicated that this is possible and shown us how to go about it. We should joyously accept his gift.

Endings and celebrations

We aren't very good at endings and partings. The forgotten stage of group development is most certainly the mourning or adjourning stage. Perhaps we are too afraid of uncertain futures to let go of the immediate past. Perhaps we have not learnt that everything is impermanent, and that is okay, because that is how it is. Have you noticed how sometimes hard-won norms and agreements become frazzled as the school year comes to an end? Things do not get finished and there is little energy for new projects. This is common but not universal, and is related to us ignoring the obvious, namely that something is about to come to an end.

A productive way to deal with this is to recap on our experience together, celebrate our achievements, make independent plans for the future and say our grateful goodbyes. We must acknowledge that we might not work together again, but will always hold a special place in our hearts for each other, and may even remain as lifelong friends or people who are overjoyed to find each other on 'Friends Reunited'. We are then free to go our ways in the world and be productive. There can be joy in goodbye. An old 'last night of camp' song is particularly helpful to sing together to remind us of the special event that is a timely ending.

> *I want to linger*
> *A little longer*
> *A little longer here with you*
> *It doesn't seem quite right*
> *That this is our last night*
> *That this is my last night with you*
> *But come September*
> *I will remember*
> *Our days of love and friendship true*
> *And as the years go by*
> *We'll know the reason why*
> *This was goodnight but not goodbye*

Conclusion

I will finish with a snapshot of a successful goodbye. This is in an educational setting, though not a formal school. It is the end of a week at a summer camp, where families meet every year to be together, to look after each other and to learn. Some of the children have been coming all their lives, and the camp contains children from birth to 18 and their parents. Two of the teachers who have been associated with the camp for some years are leaving to go abroad. We have offered goodbye gifts, sung some of the songs we learned together, reflected on and shared our favourite memories and said our heartfelt thanks. The meeting has drawn to an end, but no one has gone anywhere, we just sit perfectly quietly (including the under fives, who just respond to the genuine peace), smiling small smiles of engagement and contentment. And so it goes on, seemingly for ages. We look at each other, marvelling in the moment and not wishing to break the spell. No one rushes off to play, to get a drink or to do important chores. Eventually, some of the younger children quietly make their exit without parental influence, and gradually we all leave the room, carrying with us deeply engrained memories of important times spent together, full of wonderful learning. As the comic actor Professor Stanley Unwin would have put it: 'Oh deep joy'.

ACTION POINTS ACTION POINTS ACTION POINTS ACTION POINTS ACTION POINTS

> Use naming activities regularly.

> Make the pupils' interests and hobbies central to the classroom ethos.

> Develop class meetings.

> If you use circle time remember to allow for time to rehearse new ideas in pairs.

> Make sure everyone is included.

> Have a no put-down rule and experiment with 'you can't say you can't play'.

> Use genuinely co-operative group work at least some of the time.

> Use the jigsaw approach for projects.

> Increasingly give control to the pupils. Allow them to make mistakes and allow them the lead to develop their own ideas.

> Ensure that you review your experience, reminding yourselves what has been achieved and how everyone played a part.

> Give lots of appreciation and gratitude.

References and further reading

Dyer, A. and Lewis, J. (2001) *PSHE in the School Grounds: Learning Through Landscapes*. Crediton: Southgate.
A good compendium of activities to help your group relate to each other and to the environment.

Intrator, S. (2003) *Tuned In and Fired Up*. New Haven, CT: Yale University Press.
Inspirational accounts of heightened and exuberant moments in a high school English class.

O'Sullivan, E. (1999) *Transformative Learning*. London: Zed Books.
A well-written, informative and inspiring guide to research in approaches to deepening the educational experience.

Paley, V.G. (1992) *You Can't Say 'You Can't Play'*. Cambridge, MA: Harvard University Press.
A leading Early Years practitioner experiments with social inclusion.

16
The joy of involving pupils in their own assessment

Peter Kelly

Introduction

Teachers have long understood that assessment has a strong impact on classroom agendas and children's development. Since the 1980s researchers such as Walter Doyle in the USA and Neville Bennett and his colleagues in the UK have described how this impact can be both negative and positive. Recent initiatives in the UK such as Dylan Wiliam and Paul Black's work on assessment for learning have emphasised how assessment is most helpful when children are involved in their own assessment. Children need to be taught how to do this, but when they are, such involvement benefits their achievement across the whole curriculum. This chapter explores some of the more effective ways in which you can involve children in their own assessment.

Assessment and how children see learning

As teachers we spend a great deal of time thinking about assessment – some say too much time. Though the phrase 'you don't fatten a pig by weighing it' is overused, it also provides a helpful reminder that assessment is a means to an end and not an end in itself. As a teacher myself, in my conversations with teachers, I have found this thinking revolves around questions such as: What should we assess? When should we assess? How should we assess? What should we do with the things we find out? How do we manage this in the time available?

This is not the place to provide exhaustive answers to such questions but rather to observe that they are concerned primarily with what we as teachers do rather than with the impact of assessment on children as learners. In this chapter I will consider approaches to assessment which have a very positive influence on children's learning.

When we as teachers have exclusive responsibility for assessment in classrooms, most pupils work hard to find out what it is that will please us and act accordingly. This means children are motivated by external rewards (completing their work, pleasing their teacher, being praised) rather than the internal satisfaction which will encourage them to become lifelong learners.

Other factors are also important. In an earlier chapter in this book I suggested that performance in national tests is valued so highly that children spend a huge amount of their time in school preparing for them. Unfortunately this means many children see test performance as the sole motive for their learning at school. One way of combating this tendency is to involve children more in assessment so that they come to see assessment as a way of improving and adding to their own learning. If this is done well, if it is done consistently and if it is valued by teachers and children alike, assessment becomes a means to an end and not simply an end in itself. The rest of this chapter explores approaches which help to achieve this goal.

Involving children in assessment

The following approaches aim to support children in assessing their own learning and can be used separately or alongside others. Each approach needs time to establish as part of classroom life and become part of the way children work. Children might need to be taught how to play their part, and as their teacher you will need to show how much you value their contributions to the assessment process. However, in time they will bring benefits, although these will inevitably be much greater if similar approaches are used across the school, with the children building on and developing their own assessment skills from one class to the next.

Learning intentions

It is usual for teachers to start lessons by sharing with children their learning intentions. These indicate what they expect the children to learn in the course of that lesson. It is also considered good practice for teachers to return to these intentions at the end of the lesson and ask children questions to evaluate how successful the lesson has been in addressing the expected learning for the particular children involved. But in so doing teachers tend to take exclusive responsibility for classroom assessment.

Anticipating what children will learn is an unreliable business – classrooms, children and learning are all too complex to allow the activities teachers plan to bring about simple outcomes for all. Nevertheless, it is helpful for teachers to share their learning intentions with pupils at the start of lessons because this helps children to understand the rationale for their work and allows them to evaluate the extent to which learning tasks address the learning which they are designed to address. It therefore increases child ownership of learning tasks, and as a result children tend to be more engaged in tasks, persevering for longer and wasting less time. In consequence the quality of pupil work improves.

But it is also important that you encourage children to think about what you would like them to learn from the activities they engage in. To do this they might reflect on targets which they have set for themselves or negotiated with their teachers. By such a process we can engage children in a dialogue about their own learning, and this can help them to develop both peer-assessment skills (working with others) and self-assessment skills (working alone).

Teacher feedback and marking

Often during feedback or in marking the teacher tells the child how well he or she has done, and the child listens or reads this appraisal of their work and is then expected to remember this information so that he or she can do better in future. Again, with such an approach teachers take full responsibility for the assessment. But work can be marked in partnership with the child, and this partnership supports the learner in developing their skills of self-reflection through a collaborative dialogue. The Action Points below suggest how you can do this, and in so doing can help children to enhance their learning.

ACTION POINTS ACTION POINTS ACTION POINTS ACTION POINTS ACTION POINTS

To support children in developing skills of self-reflection, encourage them to:

> **make connections between what has been learnt and what was learnt previously;**

> **reflect on their own learning and how they went about the task;**

> **set further learning goals.**

Ways of making effective use of teacher feedback and marking

Feedback and marking are often more useful if the children know clearly what you are looking for and are best limited to just one or two objectives. Children can look for these learning points too, so start with a relatively straightforward and specific thing like a particular aspect of punctuation. When the children are familiar with this aspect they can look for more complex achievements, such as whether the characters in a story are described well. Later they might be asked to produce self-evaluations before bringing the work to you to be marked. This procedure can be encouraged using questions such as:

- What did you find easy?
- Where did you get stuck and what helped you?
- What do you need more help with?
- What are you most pleased with?
- Have you learnt anything new?

When you are marking children's work, a good rule of thumb is to give it attention in proportion to the amount of time and effort the child has contributed to the work. So a long drafted piece deserves considerable time and consideration whereas a quick practice task in mathematics deserves very little. Also, whenever possible, give your feedback orally, even if you have also written your comments down. Do not give this oral form of feedback in the form of grades; rather, highlight areas of success, suggest how the work can be improved and clearly indicate the 'next step' for the child.

Teacher–pupil conferences

Conferences are purposeful conversations between teachers and children about particular pieces of work. They can focus on negotiating an assessment of the work, with teachers modelling how children can learn from their own reflections and encouraging them to do so. Regular short one-to-one pupil–teacher conferences are often more helpful than fewer longer ones.

In managing pupil–teacher conferences it is important that you let the children lead the way. An open question might begin the process, such as: 'Tell me something about this work' or 'Tell me the story of this work'. While listening to children, you might:

- check that you have understood the sense of what the child is saying by repeating the child's phrases and asking if that is what they meant;
- ask children what they mean and whether they can then say it in a different way;
- ask for clarification on uncertainties;
- draw attention to something the child feels is relevant;
- respond to and encourage the child to say more, to go on with his or her train of thought;
- extend the sense of what the child has said by prompting the child to recognise patterns, make links and recognise the consequences and implications of their assertions;
- notice a possible error, inconsistency or problem which the child has overlooked and prompt the child to look again;
- offer reassurance, praise or other encouragement, either to celebrate what has been achieved or to motivate the child to persevere.

Conferences provide the children with models of critically reflective thinking, and the more often children engage in such conversations, the more skilled they will become and the less reliant they will be on the teacher's support. Following a conference you could ask the child to write a report on the things which arose in the conference, but later as the child becomes more experienced, you could ask them to anticipate what might come out of the conference and produce their report to act as a starting point for the conference.

These conversations bring about learning because as the children reflect on their work they clarify ideas, identify links, make new understandings and recognise and try to resolve contradictions. Thus they can change their perspectives on their work in the course of the conference. The teacher's supportive interactions help this process, although eventually the aim is that the child will be able to do the evaluation without the teacher.

Following the conference record any outcomes, including any negotiated short-term achievable targets, and how the child will be supported in working towards meeting these targets.

Peer-assessment

Peer-assessment also provides an opportunity for children to learn through carrying out assessment. It often works well in pairs, but children need to be taught how to do this. This is best done in a small group, with the teacher modelling the role of the peer assessor with a specific example of pupil work. To do this the teacher follows the process outlined in the following Action Point, making clear their thoughts and in particular the thinking processes leading to decisions and judgements. One at a time, the children can then take turns to be the teacher with the teacher supporting them.

ACTION POINT ACTION POINT ACTION POINT ACTION POINT ACTION POINT

When introducing and using peer-assessment, the children need to choose a suitable partner to discuss their work with. They then take turns to comment on each other's work. Partners should trust each other and should not include pairs where both are low-attaining children. The assessor can be called a 'response partner' and he or she:

> **talks about the other child's work in relation to specific success criteria;**

> **makes the other child feel good by pointing out what they have done well;**

> **suggests to the other child how he or she could improve the work.**

Ground rules need to be established for peer-assessment. Essential prerequisites include: partners should take turns to speak and listen carefully; there should be no interruptions; and both confidentiality and sensitivity should be maintained. Other important rules include:

- **response partners should point out what they *like* first (and highlight these) against specific (and, to begin with, very straightforward) learning intentions, while the child who produced the work listens;**
- **in all, three positive features should be identified for every one requiring improvement;**
- **after the response partner has finished, the child who produced the work can respond.**

Pupil learning diaries

Pupil learning diaries are similar to normal diaries. They can be private or public documents; they can be places where children record what they have done and describe memorable aspects of their school lives; or they can be places to think and reflect about their classroom learning experiences. When you read a child's learning diary you begin to see the world from the child's perspective and this can help you to identify individual interests and problems. At best the diary becomes a private conversation between the teacher and the child, while also providing a basis for children's developing self-evaluative skills. When they are used regularly and valued by both teachers and children, learning diaries can contribute significantly to increasing motivation, enjoyment and understanding.

Children need support in learning how to use the diaries. Training will include negotiation with the children to agree:

- who else will have access to the diaries – this is normally only the teacher, who will keep the contents of the diary confidential;
- whether the teacher will have access to the whole diary or only part of it;
- whether access should ever be shared with other children or not – if, for example, a shared anxiety is raised about, say, a fear of getting sums wrong;
- how often diaries will be written in by children – normally daily or every two days – and read by teachers – normally weekly or fortnightly;
- how the teacher should respond to their comments – normally by writing in the diary, but sometimes also by writing somewhere else or talking with the child.

Diaries normally develop through use and through the way in which they are dealt with and responded to by teachers. Where child comments are respected and acted upon, and where diaries are seen to be important by teachers, children value them and use them appropriately.

TO THINK ABOUT

It is important that you give pupil learning diaries time to work, because a rapport and sense of trust needs to develop between child and teacher. You should also think about how you should respond to personal issues or areas of concern revealed in the diary. Make sure you tell the children that you will have to seek advice or talk to others if you are overly concerned about anything revealed in the diary.

Diaries should be a two-way process: you can raise issues and thoughts with children as much as they might do with you. They also provide an opportunity for you to explore areas of understanding with children. This can be initiated by a child raising areas of confusion or misunderstanding, or you might informally ask the child about their thoughts in relation to a particular area.

Pupil portfolios

Pupil portfolios are collections of children's work, achievements and assessment information from a wide variety of contexts. They can also include records of other non-academic or out-of-school achievements, such as sports certificates. They are important because they show learning over time, thereby allowing learners to see how they have progressed, and cover a wide range of achievements which allows children, parents and teachers to get a balanced picture of strengths and areas for development. By providing this personal knowledge, portfolios can help promote positive attitudes: children gain an insight into themselves as learners, thus feel more in control of their learning and so are motivated and inspired.

During the course of the year collect together significant work from every child, in a separate folder for each, arranged chronologically to show development and progression. This work could include formative assessments such as your marking and pupil marking, pupil self-evaluations, conference records, peer-assessment discussion summaries and redrafts. Then, at particular times during the year, ask the children to consider and examine carefully the work in their portfolios. Talk to them about the process and help them to recognise and evaluate their own progress and development, and perhaps set longer-term targets for improvement in each subject area.

Conclusion

There are lots of other approaches to self-assessment and self-evaluation in schools. Some teachers ask children to use *smiley faces* to indicate how happy they are with their progress or learning in a lesson; others use a *thumbs up or down* approach in a similar way. More complex approaches can be based on *simple questionnaires* asking, for example, 'What part of the work did you find easiest or hardest'?. However, none of these encourages children to think deeply about their learning or to learn through assessment. For the first two examples, the children can respond without thinking, or more likely can give you the thumbs up simply because they want to make you happy, while questionnaires tend to produce responses which are descriptive rather than reflective and evaluative.

Without support and guidance, pupils tend to judge their own attainment and progress in relation to that of their peers. To some extent sharing learning intentions with children enables them to see how well they have achieved in relation to these intentions and not just in terms of how well they are doing in comparison with their friends and classmates. However, it is only through the kind of opportunities for 'learning conversations' described in this chapter that children can fully learn to self-assess in a critical and thoughtful manner, and thereby become self-motivated individuals who keep their enthusiasm for learning.

Further reading

Clarke, S. (2001) *Unlocking Formative Assessment: Practical Strategies for Enhancing Pupils' Learning in the Primary Classroom*. London: Hodder & Stoughton.
A useful and practical introduction to effective approaches to formative assessment.

Kelly, P. (2005) *Using Thinking Skills in the Primary Classroom*. London: Sage.
This book will provide you with more information on thinking approaches to assessment.

References

Bennett, N., Desforges, C., Cockburn, A. and Wilkinson, B. (1984) *The Quality of Pupil Learning Experiences*. London: Erlbaum.
Doyle, W. (1983) Academic work. *Review of Educational Research*, 53, 159–200.
William, D. and Black, P. (1998) *Inside the Black Box: Raising Standards Through Classroom Assessment*. London: King's College Press.
Wiliam, D. and Black, P. (2002) *Assessment for Learning: Beyond the Black Box*. Slough: NFER/Nelson.

17
Joyfully concluding
Denis Hayes

Introduction

All teachers have tales to tell about their time in school. Some experiences remain vivid and stimulate the imagination years after they happen. Others have blurred over time and reside in a far corner of the mind. Most of the stories that teachers tell concern individual children who have had a major impact on the teacher: the rascals, impossible ones and lovable ones seem to occupy a special place in our hearts. Sometimes the most difficult child finds success and goes on to achieve great things. Others fade into obscurity. In the majority of cases there is no way of knowing what has happened, for good or ill. One way and another it is the memories of children that help to confirm the fact that teaching is more than a job; it captures your heart and captivates the mind. Some memories are, however, rooted in the *people* who work alongside you: teachers, assistants, administrators, technicians, supervisors and head teachers.

I want to conclude *Joyful Teaching and Learning in the Primary School* by sharing something of my own experience in the hope that it will encourage, amuse and inspire you to grasp the nettle of the job and to recognise that you do not have to be perfect to be a successful teacher, merely 'good enough'.

After spending one year in a boys' comprehensive school in Coventry as an unqualified teacher vainly attempting to teach them Geology, I undertook an intensive primary/middle PGCE course. I then worked for nearly four years in a 5–12 first and middle school as a primary science specialist, where I cut my teeth on the job working with older primary-aged children, the majority of whom were from affluent backgrounds. There were 41 in the first class I taught and they (and some of their parents) stretched my ingenuity to the limit. Many of them relished the opportunity to write creatively and the end products, though impressive in quality, took forever to mark. Teaching had to be straightforwardly organised for the simple reason that the only way to squeeze all the children into the room was to arrange the desks (not tables) in a regular pattern.

It was during my time in this second post that I became increasingly aware that there were other smaller and noisier little people in the lower part of the school. They always seemed to have something urgent to tell you and their clothes were often daubed with paint or food stains like badges of honour. They invariably had their shoelaces flapping and used guile to be the first to hold your hand when you were on playground duty. Helpful colleagues informed me that these minors were known as 'infant children' and would one day become 'big children'.

I was fascinated by the behaviour of this species and decided to move school to find out more about their habits and customs. Consequently, I applied, and was appointed, to a post as a teacher in a large, inner-city nursery and infant school, Helsby Park Infant (pseudonym), responsible for audio-visual aids (can you imagine such a post today?).

Adjusting to a new school

In my new setting at Helsby Park there were 350 of these infant bodies fluttering around like exotic birds in a purpose-built aviary. They chirruped away non-stop and seemed incapable of standing still. I was the first male teacher ever to have been appointed to the school since it was built in the early 1950s, so I was a source of curiosity and the focus of studied attention and numerous whispered comments. Initially, there was not even a separate gents' cloakroom. Parents, children and (I suspect) colleagues were a little wary of my presence; only the head seemed confident that I could do the job. I was not so sure.

It was difficult for someone without experience of working with infant age children to adjust to the conditions. Everything seemed so small. The tables were small. The chairs were small. The meals were small. And of course the children were small. Even at that point in my career I had already worked with many different sorts of young people, both in school and in a voluntary capacity, so I did not anticipate having too many problems with these tiny tearaways. How wrong can you be! The job was among the most demanding and also the most satisfying that I had known up to that time, or since.

Lest any reader who has not worked with young children should be tempted to imagine that teaching little ones is straightforward, let me disabuse him or her of the idea straightaway. I used to stagger home exhausted, overwhelmed by the plethora of demands that the children made of me. Yet as I walked past the rows of neat terraced houses that surrounded the school, children would lean out of the windows, waving and calling a greeting. Others would dance around me as I strode along, like gambolling puppies, eagerly anticipating their walk. The experience was supremely humbling and made me feel like a king.

By contrast to all those years ago, as a trainee teacher today you will have experience of teaching a range of children in both Key Stages 1 and 2 and, perhaps, the Foundation Stage. You will learn to adjust your approach to the different age ranges while still in training and receive the advice and counsel of wiser and more experienced practitioners as you grapple with the joys and sorrows of teaching younger and older children. Unlike you, I could and did make my mistakes in the relative privacy of my own classroom.

I quickly learned that even though a few teachers occasionally moaned about the school and the head teacher they were, in fact, extremely proud to be part of such a dynamic organisation. It was very unwise to be sucked into micro-political debates or even to stand on the fringes. I found that the best course of action on such occasions was to glance with furrowed brow at my watch as if late for an appointment, and quietly slip away. You should do the same.

I also learned that it was necessary to choose allies with care. A chance remark to the 'wrong' person (albeit outwardly sympathetic) about my struggles could be transmitted to the head teacher and invoke the dreaded words, always accompanied by a fixed smile: 'Could we have a word in my office, please?' It pays to keep your counsel until you know the territory.

ACTION POINT ACTION POINT ACTION POINT ACTION POINT ACTION POINT

> Keeping up appearances and seeming to be on top of the job and contented with life forms an important element of the job. Dress smartly and colourfully but not ostentatiously and try to develop a cheery disposition. Respond positively when someone asks how you are getting on and do not get despondent if the children's behaviour unsettles you. Get things off your chest to friends or family outside school, not to colleagues.

Teaching and learning

Although teaching at the school was challenging and exhausting, it was immensely worthwhile. Most of the teaching was 'individualised'. Children read through a variety of books that were organised in level of difficulty and a child could only progress to the next book after she or he had been tested by the head or deputy and given permission to proceed. (This may seem hard to believe but it is true!) As in the majority of primary schools during the 1970s and 1980s, mathematics was taught through a small amount of whole-class teaching but mainly by working page after page through the set workbooks, which were often self-marked using answer cards that were kept on the teacher's desk. There was some use of group work and 'differentiation by task' but much of the work was personalised.

An assistant or parent took children with a weak grasp of English out of the classroom for personal tuition and what would today be referred to as 'coaching'. There was a lot of cross-curricular topic or project work, often based on local history or a science theme. Children cut, drew, painted, stuck things, mixed and spread materials to express their creativity and exercise their imaginations. Drama, PE and games were energetic, full of fun and occasionally frantic. The children skipped, swung, ran, spun, chased and celebrated the exhilaration that genuine playfulness releases.

The use of terms such as 'learning objectives' and 'targets' and 'achievement books' was unknown, yet most of the children progressed well. Standards of reading were high by any measure; the majority of children were numerate and they were certainly never short of ideas and things to say.

The only timetabled events were when the hall was required for physical activity and booking to watch specified TV programmes in a dedicated area. If a session was proceeding nicely and the children were engaged with their learning and concentration levels were being maintained, a 'lesson' could run for half a day. Teachers milked pupil enthusiasm and took close account of class mood. If the children were obviously restless and the session felt like trudging across a muddy field, the teacher would change tack and give children a 'settling down' straightforward task to do before recommencing the original work. If they were keen to continue, the teacher extended the session beyond the normal break.

As a new teacher you will find that most primary schools adhere to a fairly strict timetable based on subject areas, though much less so in the Foundation Stage. In the upper stages of Key Stage 2 the classes often combine for English and mathematics (particularly), dividing up the pupils into ability groups to facilitate more targeted teaching. However, in other areas of the curriculum and in problem-solving sessions it is worth looking for opportunities to 'bend' the conventions a little after appropriate consultation with the host teacher and allow children to explore a topic more thoroughly than a single 'lesson' allows for.

In the schools at which I taught, collaboration in most areas of learning (the word 'subjects' was used only in secondary schools until the mid-1980s) was commonplace, apart from in mathematics and English, and in all other subjects teachers had to design their own lessons. The internet, downloading of pre-designed worksheets and glossy government literature with 'advice and guidance' about preferred teaching methods or strategies were some twenty years away. National Curriculum tests (known as SATs by most people today) and league tables of performance did not exist. There were rigorous inspections of schools by Her Majesty's Inspectors (HMI), but Ofsted had not been created. Advisers from the local education authority provided training courses and advice, but unlike today they were 'critical friends' rather than 'regulators'.

Record-keeping of pupil progress largely consisted of noting which book a child had read, the occasions on which he or she read aloud to an adult and when the child changed 'up' to the next level of maths book. Reports were once per year and brief. Teachers did what they believed to be in the best interests of their children, yet the head's word was law. Teaching tended to be a complex amalgam of high formality and random opportunism. High-quality displays festooned the school and most classrooms (including my own); the sound of children singing echoed down corridors. And it was here, in this pulsating environment, that I met the unforgettable Mrs Honeybee.

Mrs Honeybee was a *classroom assistant*, not a teaching assistant, learning support teacher, special needs assistant or any other title. She was a plain and ordinary classroom assistant and proud of it. Mrs Honeybee mixed paints for children, sharpened pencils, boiled the kettle for cups of tea, sold biscuits at breaktime and put up displays around the school. She, and the two other full-time assistants, heard children read, shared playground duties with teachers, mended damaged books, washed soiled knickers and served behind stalls at school events.

TO THINK ABOUT

Teaching assistants are your colleagues, not your servants. Many of them have considerable expertise and experience to offer, much of which remains unused. The sight of a well-qualified assistant being reduced to 'shushing' the children during an interactive session or carrying out trivial 'repair and mend' tasks is an affront to their integrity and competence.

Mrs Honeybee had worked at the school for many years. She lived locally and knew something useful about every parent; she sensed that trouble was brewing before it happened and spent much of her time alerting teachers to 'goings on' that they would otherwise never have known about. It was Mrs Honeybee who spotted two six-year-olds sneaking into school during a sports afternoon and caught them red-handed retrieving stolen money that they had cleverly hidden in the 'bottle top' tin. It was Mrs Honeybee who intuitively knew when a teacher needed a consoling word or a warning about the head teacher's mood. And it was Mrs Honeybee who, after my six- and seven-year-olds had completed what I considered to be a masterpiece of a dinosaur picture painted on card over nine feet (three metres) high for displaying in the hall, along with eleven other similar effigies from the other classes, came to me quietly after school to offer some necessary but unwelcome feedback on the merits of the artistic endeavour. (It is important to know that the head, a wonderfully committed lady, was a great enthusiast for displays around the school as a means of stimulating language in a school that was over 75 per cent Gujarati-speaking.)

CASE STUDY 17.1

Mrs Honeybee

Mrs Honeybee came to the door of the classroom as I stood proudly surveying the dinosaur creation that lay across the floor, a few prints from the soles of children's shoes along its edges bearing testimony to the practical problems of 34 infants shuffling past it on their way home. Enter Mrs Honeybee.

Well, what do you think, Mrs Honeybee? They've really done well and it's their own work, not mine, I declared proudly. Mrs Honeybee did not respond with her usual gush of approval.

Well, she paused, her strong Brummie dialect in bottom gear, *it's nice* (pause again) *but I don't think that the head'll be very satisfied somehow*. Alarm shows on my face. I hear my own Birmingham accent pulsing as I try to suppress a rising sense of panic.

Why is that, Mrs Honeybee?

Mrs Honeybee stood rigid for a few seconds while she thought about her response. I recall gazing into her ever-so-slightly anxious face as she considered how best to break the news to me. She sighed gently and then spoke slowly and carefully, as if revealing a closely guarded secret: *Some of the babbies (younger children) have done a better one than this*. I choked for a moment, my self-assurance draining through the soles of my feet.

But they did it themselves, I heard myself stuttering. *I thought that's what the head wanted.*

Mrs Honeybee half-smiled and her generous face creased in a suppressed grin. *Oh yes, she does ... but the other teachers make sure that when they do theirs ... well ...* Her voice trailed off.

I knew instinctively what she was saying. The other teachers made sure that there was a considerable amount of 'adult contribution' to their children's efforts to ensure the highest possible standard of end product. I nodded slowly as the penny dropped.

What do you think I should do, Mrs Honeybee?

I saw her hesitate again, anxious not to be seen as interfering, yet keen to help me out of the mess, so I gave her the words.

Do you think that I should do it again, myself, after school?

Again the mysterious smile. I could almost hear her thinking aloud: 'The lad might survive yet.'

Well, if I wuz you, I think I might do just that.

Thanks, Mrs Honeybee.

That's okay. Try not to stay too late. I must go 'ome and get me 'usband's tea or 'e'll think I've deserted 'im. She made her exit and did not look back.

TO THINK ABOUT
TO THINK ABOUT

How much should teachers intervene? When should children be simply allowed to 'get on with it' and how much skills training should precede the main activity? How might TAs be involved? How will you inform them?

The joy of expediency

After Mrs Honeybee's intervention I began immediately to gather together the necessary materials for the forgery: paints, card, scissors, adhesive tape, glue, tissue paper, beads, cardboard rolls and the rest. After keeping well out of sight until the head and rest of the staff had gone home, I set to work in earnest. It now seems incredible that the head used to say that anyone still in school after half-past four was obviously not tired enough to go home so could not have done a proper day's work. She had a point. I finished my skulduggery just before six o'clock, making sure that I included one or two 'child-like' blemishes just in case someone questioned its authenticity. The displays were to be assembled the following day. I had to get it right first time. There was no room for error.

The following morning I crept into the classroom early to examine my masterpiece. In the fresh light of day I saw a number of glaring faults and hurriedly touched them up, being careful not to put on the paint and glue too thickly for fear they would not dry before the monstrosity was hung up at the start of school. After registration, selected children from each class carried the dinosaurs across to the hall like spoils from a big-game hunt, teachers and assistants fussing around and directing them. Painstakingly, my children followed suit. Why was I holding my breath?

Mrs Honeybee and the other assistants spent the whole day assembling the montage in the main hall. After school I casually walked over to see how things were going. The spectacle was nearly complete and, yes, there was 'our' dinosaur on the wall peeping out from a background of jungle reeds, looking much less imposing than when it had been on the classroom floor but acceptably good nonetheless. Some of my artistic colleagues had produced far more imaginative creations, but mine was not a disaster by any measure. A large number of children and parents were passing through the hall and I saw several of my own class pointing excitedly at 'their' picture. I swallowed hard, but none of them spotted the counterfeit. The head wandered across to me.

Nice work, Denis, she smiled. *Your class did pretty well*.

Yes, I croaked feebly, *they certainly didn't let me down*. (I blush with shame as I write this – unprofessional or what!)

I saw Mrs Honeybee out of the corner of my eye, pinning up giant labels with information about the creatures. Would she betray me? Would she give the game away by tittering or making a cryptic comment? I should have known better. Her face was calm; her voice was steady as she chattered away to the children around her. How she loved them. How they adored her. And so did I. She was the salt of the earth.

ACTION POINT ACTION POINT ACTION POINT ACTION POINT ACTION POINT

> Learn from my unfortunate experience. Seek advice before the event, not during or after it. There is no shame in admitting a lack of knowledge. Do not allow yourself to be placed in a position where you might be embarrassed or need to rely on someone else to rescue you from a pending disaster.

Conclusion

In the thirty years and more since the event described above, the role of assistants has changed considerably. I have changed, too. I'm older, less lofty in my opinions, balding and a bit overweight. If still alive, Mrs Honeybee will now be well into her eighties. Her modern-day contemporaries (TAs) are rightly seen as an increasingly important part of every school's teaching and learning programme. There are now National Occupational Standards (NOS) for assistants to negotiate as part of their professional training and TAs are often mentioned in the education press. Their changing role and the way that Higher Level Teaching Assistants (HLTA) are now employed in classrooms as supporting teachers ensures that they will be the focus of attention for years to come.

To the outside observer, schools have changed beyond recognition. New buildings with magnificent technological facilities, staffed by large numbers of adults, shelves bulging from the weight of government circulars, curriculum documents, policy decisions and the latest big idea have become a familiar sight. So, too, have security fences, electronic protection systems and identity cards.

Yet the heart of primary education remains largely unchanged. Adults and children strive to gain knowledge, understand better the world in which they live and recognise their unique place in it. Children still learn; teachers still help them to do so. Relationships and motivation remain central to the educative endeavour. The vast majority of parents want only the best for their children, academically and socially. The world and society remain far from perfect but you have the privilege of affirming the infinite value of each individual and promoting his or her sense of responsibility.

In the midst of the stresses and strains that undoubtedly accompany this most demanding of professions, you should find time in your imagination to pause and listen to the children you teach call out their greeting as you walk the streets. Their bright faces and fervency – even the naughty ones – will stimulate your mind and memory long after concerns about tutors, paperwork, targets and political interference are long forgotten. And you will know that your decision to teach because you wanted a job that would really make a difference to children's lives was the right one.

Teaching and learning is not always joyful, but the knowledge that you are doing one of the most important jobs on earth should be sufficient incentive to persevere. And let's hope that you find joy in your colleagues, too – especially if they demonstrate the caring qualities shown by a wonderful lady called Mrs Honeybee.

Further reading

Hargreaves, A. and Fullan, M. (1998) *What's Worth Fighting for in Education?* Maidenhead: Open University.
This classic book helps the reader to rediscover the passion and moral purpose that makes teaching and learning an exciting enterprise.

Jacklin, A., Griffiths, V. and Robinson, C. (2006) *Beginning Primary Teaching*. Maidenhead: Open University.
This affirming and encouraging book helps primary teachers to understand their early professional development and learning, and to reflect on their classroom practice.

Rogers, B. (2006) *I Get By with a Little Help*. London: Sage.
The author draws on his wide experience to emphasise that colleague support can and does make a difference to individual teachers and whole-school culture.

Index

Added to a page number 'f' denotes a figure and 't' denotes a table.

critical 56, 72–3
  emotions at the heart of 71–2
  encouragement of 19
  geographical 48
  inclusive 114
  role in education process 70–1
thinking journals 24
time management 7
trainee teachers 2
Training and Development Agency (TDA) 4
transformative learning 127
Tuned In and Fired Up 127–8
tutors 2

U
ubiquitous learning 10

V
value beliefs 71
visual resources, geography 46t
visualisation 91, 92f
vocabulary, geography 48

W
Warnock Report (1978) 114
weather, overcoming difficulties presented
    by 57–8
What is naughty? 24–5
What? questions 39
What's under the rug? 21–2
Why? questions 39
Write On! 58